a scandalous
beauty

a scandalous *beauty*

THE **ARTISTRY** OF GOD
AND THE **WAY** OF THE CROSS

THOMAS SCHMIDT

Brazos Press
A Division of Baker Book House Co
Grand Rapids, Michigan 49516

Published by Brazos Press
a division of Baker Book House Company
P.O. Box 6287, Grand Rapids, MI 49516–6287

Printed in the United States of America

Library of Congress Cataloging-in-Publication Data

Schmidt, Thomas, 1955–
    A scandalous beauty : the artistry of God and the way of the Cross /
Thomas Schmidt.
      p.   cm.
    ISBN 1-58743-017-7
    1. Jesus Christ—Crucifixion—Meditations. I. Title.
BT453 .S48   2002
232.96—dc21   2001037315

For current information about all releases from Brazos Press, visit our web site:
http://www.brazospress.com

contents

Why This Book   7

1. What Luck   9

A contemporary retelling of the stories of all of the disciples and the thief on the cross suggests that God works through the circumstances of normal lives.

2. The Womb, the Tomb, and the Curtained Room   18

Mysterious and connected barriers are penetrated at key points in Jesus' life, revealing an underlying pattern in the Gospels.

3. The Man Who Would Be God   31

Mark's story of the crucifixion is a deliberate attempt to mock the Roman triumphal procession practiced by Nero and others to deify themselves.

4. God's Pyramid Scheme   38

The death of Jesus perfects the logic of the Pharisees' idea of atonement, which suggests that greater value accrues for greater suffering and greater innocence.

5. Jesus Goes to Therapy   52

A mock counseling session draws attention to modern misunderstanding of the emotions and motives of Jesus, particularly moments of pain such as his cry from the cross.

6. The God in the Garden   66

Jesus' appearance to Mary in John 20 is an example of God's refusal to remain entombed in human limitations.

7. Return of the Living Dead   75

The caricature we create of Paul contrasts with the reality revealed in his letters, especially the extraordinary empathy displayed in passages like 2 Corinthians 1:3–11.

8. On Death and Power and One Old Lady   86

Mabel, an old woman who persevered in the face of extraordinary suffering, demonstrates the kind of power described in Paul's letters.

9. *T* and Sympathy   102

In Hebrews 2:14, a literary device, multiple repetition of the Greek letter *tau,* presents the cross as God's answer to human suffering.

10. Eternity: No Day at the Beach   114

Revelation 21:1 and the sea imagery of the Apocalypse signify God's restoration of order from human chaos and rebellion.

Acknowledgments   127

why this book

MY GRANDMOTHER DID NOT TEACH ME TO PRAY, NOR did she know anything about theology. She prayed, though—out loud, in German, in a singsong voice, sitting in a chair in the living room with a Bible on her lap. I was supposed to be in bed, fast asleep, but I peeked once. Mostly I would just lay there and listen.

There was one phrase I heard over and over, like a title over every paragraph of prayer: *O lieber Heiland.* She spoke those words with passion, sometimes drawing the *O* out like a cry of pain. I had no idea what it meant. A "high land"—heaven, maybe? And I had no clue what a "leeber" was. But there was one other word I would always listen for in her prayer, and it was to me like a magic spell, offering peace and opening the gate to dreamland. It was my name. After so many *lieber Heilands* and a great number of other unintelligible words, eventually I would hear that one word: *Tommy.* Then I could sleep.

Now I can pray. This isn't about goodness, although she was good. It isn't about truth, although she clung to the true. It is about beauty. It is about a love that touched my imagination.

This book isn't about morality: I have nothing to preach to anyone. This book isn't about truth: I have nothing to prove to anyone. This book is about the artistry, the imagination, the beauty of a particular event: the death of Jesus. That event has implications for theology and morality, but other people and other books explore those implications. The essays here all touch upon the death of Jesus, and they are organized canonically (that is, they follow the order of the New Testament writings), but they do not build an argument. Rather, they explore different avenues in the same neighborhood. It is a neighborhood Christians rarely visit, where pictures and metaphors touch the imagination, where God expresses his *style*. Most of us are more familiar, and maybe more comfortable, with preachers and professors, and we'd like God to be like that. Heaven forbid that God should turn out to be an *artist*.

But there it is. The ratio of poetry to pure doctrine in the Bible is at least fifty to one, and most of the rest—including the life and teaching of Jesus—consists of stories and parables. Why isn't it all spelled out for us more clearly? At times it seems as if God is in another room, the voice is muffled or the language is foreign, and we aren't quite sure if we can hear our own name being spoken. Artists can be so exasperating. They can also touch us, invite us, entice us into discovering for ourselves what no amount of preaching or explaining could.

If my own discoveries, my own choices of words, can convey something of God's artistry, then I have grown closer to the image in which I was made, and my grandmother's prayers are being answered.

O lieber Heiland. O precious Savior. I never forgot those words, and eventually I acquired the knowledge to translate them. Now I want them to be the titles of paragraphs again—not only of my prayers, but of my life.

My grandmother's name was Susanna. I named my daughter after her. Together these two opened doors for me into God's mystery and artistry in life and in death. I dedicate this book to the two of them, and to the hope of our meeting, beyond imagining, at the end of beauty.

1

what luck

IT IS AN APRIL MORNING IN OXNARD, CALIFORNIA ON ONE
of those roads coming up toward the freeway from the
ocean, dividing huge flat fields, at this time of year full of
strawberries. It's early, and low coastal clouds hang over
the fields. Two brothers, Pedro and Andujar, are bent over,
picking, having picked more berries already this morning
than you or I could pick in a week. That's what they do.

This morning the brothers work their way to the end of
a row, within earshot of the road, just at the moment that
a pickup truck slows down and the driver leans out the window. He's someone they recognize, Haysoos (that's pho-
netic Spanish for "Jesus," you understand), a gardener from
Ventura they met once but know little about except that
some old ladies think he is some kind of saint. So there is
Haysoos just as they get to the end of this long row of strawberries, and he leans out the window and says, "Hop in the
back, and I will make you pick crates full of people."

Now, that is a pretty amazing thing to say, but what is
more amazing is that Pedro and Andujar step out of the
end of the row and get into the back of the truck. And that's
not all. At this very moment, on the other side of the road,
there just happens to be parked a big flatbed truck in which
there is another pair of brothers, Juan and Santiago. They

are not migrant workers; they have their own hundred-acre field, and they are standing in the back of their father's truck with a couple of other workers organizing the crates to put out on the rows for the pickers. Haysoos leans out of the other side of the cab and says to Juan and Santiago simply, "Get in my truck." And they do.

So off they go, Haysoos driving and these four guys in the back, plus a lawnmower and two big trash cans, and they get on the 101 freeway and drive north thirty miles until they take the Salinas Street exit in Santa Barbara and head for the roundabout at the bottom of Barker Pass, a big hill leading up into the Monticeto hills. This is where I come into the story, because it just happens that this is the same moment I'm driving from my house in downtown Santa Barbara, and I get to that roundabout just about three seconds *after* Haysoos and company. This is bad news. Those who live here know, and those who don't can imagine, that when you find yourself driving up a hill behind a pickup with a lawnmower and two trash cans and four Mexican guys looking at you with no expression on their faces, you will have a lot of time to think on the way up that hill, because those trucks have an extra gear: fourth, third, second, first, and Anglo In A Big Hurry Right Behind.

So I'm frustrated. Here I have lectures to give, books to write, meetings to attend, and instead I'm stuck . . . following Haysoos.

I have to confess that at this point I utter a four-letter word that Christians are taught never to use. More specifically, a word that ends with the letters u-c-k. "What luck," I cry. You see, somewhere along the way I was instructed that words like "luck" and "lot" and "chance" should never be part of a Christian's vocabulary, for if God is in control of our world and our lives, nothing happens by chance. So if someone says "good luck," I should remind myself that I don't believe in luck; I believe in God.

But then a couple of years ago I read an interesting play by Charles Williams entitled *The Death of Good Fortune.* Through the voice of Mary, the principal character, Williams claims that since Christ came, there is still luck, or what people called fate and fortune in ancient times. The difference is that now, because of Christ, all luck is good luck. That is, God weaves patterns complex beyond our imagining to allow each of us to know his love and mercy in a way perfectly suited to our own circumstances. The timing, the people, all the details of our lives constitute parts of God's message of grace. Could that really be true? How could we know?

Interesting question, I thought, then I looked ahead and there were Pedro and Andujar and Juan and Santiago and the two trash cans, we hadn't even gotten halfway up the hill yet, and they were showing no signs of turning off. I gazed past them up to the cab and noticed the large pair of fuzzy dice bouncing around under the rearview mirror, and it seemed like every way they turned they always added up to seven, and that got me thinking about luck again.

I remember years ago seeing the film *Jurassic Park* with some fellow academic types. In the film, Jeff Goldblum plays a scientist who talks about something called "chaos theory," which describes the unpredictability of results. After the film I asked one of my friends, a professor of mathematics, to explain chaos theory to me. He was more than happy to do so, and of course I didn't understand his explanation. But he used an illustration that came back to me on my way up Barker Pass.

Meteorologists say that weather systems are triggered and change directions according to tiny little movements, as small as a flock of birds taking off, that begin chain reactions so enormous as to make a hurricane's arrival and intensity impossible to predict with precision. At any one time scientists can tell us where a storm is, how fast it is moving, and the direction it is heading, but they are rarely correct about its destination. I remember once when a hurricane was heading for the Carolina coast, but it didn't do what Hurricane Andrew did some years ago. Instead, it fizzled out over the ocean, and if it was a disaster, it was only so to the newspeople who sent all that expensive equipment to bring the destruction into our living rooms. There was poor Dan Rather in a helicopter flying around pointing out a few trees that had blown down and a lot of houses that hadn't blown down. The big story was foiled— by a flock of birds, perhaps. I thought about that, and I thought about the fact that a flock of birds sometimes takes off because a single bird takes off—scientists call it "infectious behavior"—and maybe that bird is disturbed because of a single itchy feather. What's a meteorologist to do? Then I thought about the Gospel of Matthew, where the Lord says for us not to worry because not a sparrow falls to the ground (or flaps its wings, I suppose) apart from the will of God, so God must certainly be involved in all the details of our lives, which are far more important to him than sparrows.

Now most of us consider that a pleasant thought, but we don't think of it having much to do with us, and we certainly don't apply it to the Gospel story. We normally associate Jesus' ministry with acts of great power, miracles, God setting aside what we would call "luck" or the normal course of events and instead acting supernaturally to send his Son into our world to suffer on our behalf and then to raise him from the dead. None of this sounds much like God making use of circumstances or luck, good luck or otherwise. It sounds like God taking charge of things. But there is something else there in the story, something less obvious. That is the perspective, the circumstances, of the people who gained eternally by the presence of Jesus in their world.

What were the chances at a human level that things would turn out as they did? What was it that made Pedro and Andujar choose a certain row of berries at a certain time and pick at a certain rate so that they would be at the end of that row when a certain pickup drove by? What were the odds that at that very moment there would be another pair of brothers in a truck on the opposite side of the road also within earshot? Think of the uncountable number of choices, escapes from accident, all their lives, that made it possible for those four even to be there on that day. And then, the most amazing set of circumstances of all, what was happening in each of their hearts that they would all be not only at just that place but at just that point in their lives that they would be willing to go at that moment almost as if they had been waiting for it? How did they know, how could anybody know, that this pickup was being driven by the Savior of the world? For all this to happen, God would have to be more than a God of compelling sayings like "I will make you pick crates full of people." He would have to be a God of details, all the details of the lives of these men. A God of miracles and hurricanes, yes—but also a God of sparrows.

Well, by now I was more than halfway up Barker Pass, and these guys in front of me were moving with all the speed and facial enthusiasm that makes you think they are going to be killed at the top of the hill. I remembered that thought when I was writing this, and it struck me as a kind of coincidence in light of what I learned about that Haysoos guy later that summer.

It all had to do with another Latino from Oxnard whose name I forgot but whose story I heard from a former student of mine who is now a prison chaplain. This Latino had been nothing but trouble from the time anybody could remember, and by the time he was twenty he was a gang banger and heading for bigger trouble. Sometimes he thinks of himself as a religious guy—at least he believes in God, thanks to the influence of his saintly mother—but most of the time he thinks of himself as a tough guy. One fine day he decides to try his hand at robbing a bank in nearby Ventura. He picks a bank that is undergoing some remodeling, figuring things will be a little confused in the lobby, and he walks up to a teller and pulls a pistol. But he is a bit nervous, and after she fills a bag with cash and hands it over to him he backs into a sign that describes a new interest rate on minimum balance checking. This surprises him (the sign, not the interest rate), he jerks, and by some chance the gun goes off.

Now it just happens that the remodeling in the bank consisted of replacing the mahogany teller counters with granite teller counters, and that bullet heads straight for the side of the teller window, where two days earlier it would have lodged in wood but today it bounces off granite and lands just above the heart of the bank teller, killing her almost instantly. What luck. So our friend the thief—now also a murderer—runs out of the bank and heads for his car to get to his mama's trailer in Oxnard and from there to L.A. or Tijuana, where he plans to lay low for a while. But what he doesn't figure on is that the '72 Impala he borrowed for the job has expired plates, and when he jogs around the corner with a smoking gun in his pocket and a bag of money in his hand, there is a policeman standing there writing out a ticket. What luck. So he goes to jail, and his court-appointed attorney manages to put off the inevitable a few times by delaying tactics and appeals, but in the end he is sentenced by the toughest judge in the county because the delays push the sentencing into the vacation period of the most lenient judge in the county. What luck.

So they take him to death row, and just before the end he decides that being a tough guy is not so good after all, he begins to think a lot about his mama and what she believes. He calls for the prison chaplain, my former student, and guess what the prison chaplain finds when he arrives? He finds three cells with three prisoners who have just been moved there to wait for execution: the guy I've been describing, another guy pretty much like him, and a gardener from Camarillo who apparently did something terrible—my friend couldn't remember quite what. When he arrives the gardener is being hassled by the other inmate, and our unlucky thief is sticking up for him. He tells the other inmate to back off and says, "Listen, we've done bad things and we are getting what's coming to us, but I don't think this guy could have done what they are saying he did. I think he's a saint." And he turns to the gardener and says, "Hey, you put in a good word for me with Mary, okay?" And the gardener says, "I will see you in heaven today."

What luck. To end up on death row the very day that the person in the cell next to you happens to be the Savior of the world. Don't you think the thief on the cross was the one thief in the world who would benefit from being at that place at that moment? He was worth much more than a sparrow, and all his wing flaps over the course of a lifetime, all the little details of his fall, led him to be raised to a cross that day so that he could be forgiven and given life at the moment of his death.

We read such stories in the Bible, and we usually derive from them truths about the character of God—in this case, the truth that God is willing to forgive us no matter what we do, whenever we turn to him, even at the last minute. But there are truths about people there too, people like you and me whose encounters with God, whose life directions, were derived not from Bible study or insightful counseling but simply from combinations of circumstances that at the level of outside observation seemed coincidental, but at the level of those people's perception seemed to be the call of God. They took those words about sparrows personally.

As for us, we are all of us something between disciples and thieves. Life moves along, things happen to us. Perhaps we avoid four-letter words like "luck," preferring to describe our circumstances as fortunate or unfortunate. But if we take Jesus seriously when he speaks of sparrows, then the events of our lives that on the surface seem random occurrences are, to a deeper vision, part of a very complex plan to make each of us people of grace. Some see more of the plan than others, none of us sees all of it, and what we do see we don't see very clearly. I suspect that the difference between us is not our luck; it is our seeing. How much do we see with God's sight?

One of those greeting card sayings that you might have read is that life is what happens to us while we are making plans for the future. Maybe God's will is what happens to us while we are busy looking for God's will—or while we are merely busy. Maybe the still small voice we are waiting to hear is already whispering in the details of our lives— especially the details we wish would go away and leave us alone. The slow pickups in life that seem to show up just in front of us when we most want a smooth, fast road.

I have a close friend, a wise, learned professional counselor, who once listened to me describe a painful dilemma, a situation that appeared to face me with great loss no matter what I chose to do. An absolute stumper that all of my knowledge of Scripture, my experience in counseling, and the wisdom of all the sages I've studied left me powerless to resolve. My friend heard me out, and when I had finished I expected the usual response of a friend who is also a professional: empathy, coupled with good questions and feedback. Instead, he sat silently for almost a minute, and then he shook his head and with a tone in his voice something like wonder, or maybe even envy, he said, "Wow! God must have something extraordinary in mind for you!"

Maybe the difference between people is not their luck but their seeing. Maybe the still small voice you are waiting to hear is already whispering in the details of your life.

What is it whispering? I can barely hear it for me, and I certainly can't hear it for you. It whispers so close to your ear that no one else can hear it. You know your pain, or whatever it is that fills your mind in quiet moments. I only know that there are some circumstances in your life, like there are in mine, that you could see as "unfortunate," or your lot in life, or something you are stuck with, or somebody else's fault, or just a bad break . . . or the love of God who is whispering for you to look, look again, look harder, and see something new. Some new opportunity to know God's infinite and infinitely complex and amazingly individual grace. Some new chance to forgive and be forgiven. Some new possibility to learn love, especially for someone who doesn't seem the least bit lovable. Something extraordinary God has in mind. What will you see when you look? Is this parable of mine also yours?

One day in April I was stuck behind a slow truck. I was looking. I was looking at four guys in the back; I was looking at the lawnmower and the trash cans, and I was looking at big fuzzy dice bouncing around below the mirror that always seemed to add up to seven. What luck. What I didn't look at in that truck was the rearview mirror itself. I wonder now what I might have seen. Whose eyes might those have been looking back at me?

17

2

the womb, the tomb, and the curtained room

THEATER CRITICS WHO DIDN'T LIKE THE REST OF THE play called it a cheap special-effects trick. "Overly dramatic," they said, "a distraction from the more important themes of the work." Positive reviewers thought the effect was "somehow profoundly mysterious," but their speculation about its meaning was somehow profoundly clueless. Audience members leaving the theater said things like, "Wow, that was cool," "How did they do that?" and "Wanna get some coffee now?"

What happened was this. Near the end of the play, the hero is dying, stage front, behind him the enormous blue velvet stage curtain. He exhales one last time, the sound of his final breath amplified by the theater sound system. And just at that moment, with a terrible ripping sound, the entire stage curtain tears in two from top to bottom. A Roman centurion walks in from stage right, stands over the hero, faces the audience, and delivers his only line: "Surely this was the Son of God." The audience, still buzzing over the curtain business, doesn't pay much attention to the soldier.

But they should. The playwright has been setting this up the whole time, and like any good playwright, he is interweaving material not only from within his own play but from a dramatic tradition that goes way back—back further, maybe, than even he is aware. So what if the audience doesn't get it all, and so what if the critics are divided? The point of this drama is that they are all *participants,* whether or not they know it, whether or not they pick up enough clues even to call it comedy or tragedy.

This chapter is about the clues in the Gospels—or in stage terms, the *cues.* At one level, they are simple, straightforward directions for the audience: here is what's happening and here is how you should react; he's the Son of God and you should love him. At another level, these cues entice us into places of mystery where we are awed by the complexity and connectedness of images and events. The metaphor of a tapestry, the backside of which reveals the technique of the artist, is more than fitting, since the historical curtain in question was richly embroidered. The view from the other side shows a craft of incomparable richness and depth.

The Mystery of the Veil

Most of us are able to conjure an image of the ancient temple of the Jews from Bible illustrations or films. Contemporary accounts describe a glorious structure of white marble, decorated in gold, set like a jewel among acres of courtyards on the temple mount in Jerusalem. The temple itself was about a hundred feet long, forty feet wide, and seventy feet high, with a somewhat taller and wider facade. Inside a large open vestibule was the main room, and at the far end a smaller room known as the holy of holies, where only the high priest could enter, and then only on the annual Day of Atonement.

Between the main room of the temple and the holy of holies was a curtain, not a door. Since passage between the two rooms symbolized entry into God's presence, it was natural for early Christians to think of Jesus as the one who *enters the inner shrine behind the curtain . . . a forerunner on our behalf* (Heb. 6:19–20; 10:19–20). As a result, many assume that the curtain torn at Jesus' death was that curtain between the temple and the holy of holies. One problem, of course, is that this curtain could not be seen from outside the building, while the story seems to imply that the event was observable—even that the centurion who called Jesus the Son of God was responding directly to his observation of its tearing (Matt. 27:54). This brings more questions. Why would the Gospel quote a Roman soldier at such a crucial moment? Why would he or anyone interpret the torn temple curtain in this way? Would he mean what Christians mean by "Son of God"? And how could he or anyone see inside the temple from the place of Jesus' crucifixion?

Today, tourists looking for Golgotha visit a lump of rock covered by an enormous altar inside the Church of the Holy Sepulcher or the nearby Protestant alternative, a wall of rock that looks pretty spooky until you learn that it got that way in the middle ages when it was a rock quarry. Whatever historical claims these sites have, both are behind and below and therefore out of visual range of the ancient temple. There is some evidence, however, that the actual place of crucifixion was on the Mount of Olives directly east and above the temple across the narrow Kidron Valley. This would be just like the Romans, to make sure the Jews observed Roman justice from their temple; and it also means that the place where executions took place afforded a commanding view of the temple itself. But what of the temple curtain? The answer to this question involves some old but neglected information about the temple. In front of the sanctuary or main room of the temple hung an enormous curtain, about fifty feet high and thirty feet wide. This curtain, hanging inside the open temple vestibule, would have been visible from a considerable distance, and the best view would have been from the Mount of Olives. That may help with the mystery of its tearing as an observable event, but what of its significance?

According to the first-century Jewish historian Josephus, the great temple curtain was embroidered to represent "the panorama of the heavens." In other words, it symbolized the sky, and the sky was understood as a barrier between this world and the abode of God. The tearing of the temple curtain, then, has to do with God's Spirit moving in or out of the world. Interestingly, the only other place that this graphic verb "to tear apart" occurs in Mark's Gospel is in the opening chapter, where the sky opens at Jesus' baptism. And what happens immediately afterward? God's Spirit "descends" and a heavenly voice announces, *You are my son* (Mark 1:10). Of course this leaves us wondering why at the end of Jesus' career we get the voice of a Roman soldier instead of God (more on that later), but the parallels between the two events are too obvious to ignore. The connections between these announcements open the door—or should we say the skylight? to closer scrutiny of such imagery here and elsewhere in the Gospels. What emerges is a fascinating pattern of "divine penetration," where key events in the career of Jesus are signaled by movement through richly symbolic physical barriers.

The Sky God in Ancient Times

Virtually every religion begins with a supreme sky deity. This god is generally distant, passive, and abstract. Eventually he is supplanted by a creator-god who is more in touch with the earth. In the Greek tradition, creation begins with Ouranos the sky god, who creates and is at the same time the dwelling place of the other gods. The word *ouranos* is in fact the Greek word for sky, and Ouranos is eventually abstracted from a god to the place name for sky or heaven. His creations Zeus and Hera populate Olympus with the colorful cast of divinities familiar to us from ancient Greek literature.

But what of the Jews? In the Hebrew Scriptures, it is very common to depict God as spatially "up." He is referred to as "Most High" over thirty times, he is commonly called the one *who rides upon the clouds* (Ps. 68:4), and he is often approached from the tops of mountains (Exod. 3:1; Ezek. 40:2). The sky itself is understood as the barrier between humanity and God. It is natural that a culture developing from nomadic people who contemplated the star-strewn night sky would describe heaven as a garment or tent. God *stretches out the heavens like a curtain, and spreads them like a tent to live in* (Isa. 40:22). Tents were made of skins, and so the sky may be rent or unstitched, rolled as a scroll, or it may contain windows. Most simply, of course, heaven simply "opens" as in the opening at the beginning of the book of Ezekiel, *the heavens were opened, and I saw visions of God.* This imagery remained even as the Jews' picture of the cosmos developed to the point of a seven-layered heaven. The lowest level, seen from below as the vault of the sky and separating man from the waters above—and ultimately God, high above—was called by the Latin word for skin, *velum.*

All of this helps us to understand why the Jews would place an image of the sky, in the form of a great curtain, between the vestibule and the sanctuary of the temple. To move horizontally into God's house was to pass in a symbolic sense vertically into the upper heavens. The vestibule itself was a staging place for the activity within the temple and was every bit as holy.

The Spirit Wind

In accounts of Jesus' baptism, the heavens are rent or opened, the Spirit descends upon Jesus from heaven as a dove, and the phenomenon is followed immediately by the voice of God proclaiming Jesus as Son. Earlier I drew attention to Mark's version, where the same graphic verb of tearing is used for the sky at Jesus' baptism and the temple curtain at Jesus' crucifixion. That is not the only connection between the two passages.

In Hebrew, "wind" and "spirit" are the same word. Many Old Testament stories portray God's presence or Spirit in the form of a wind or its powerful effects, and the spirit or breath of a person is understood in the same terms. So when Jesus breathes his last *with a loud cry,* we should understand this cry not as a wail but as an act of great power, a mighty Spirit-wind that rips open the sky—that is, the temple curtain. God's Spirit is not moving down, as in the baptism story, but up from Jesus through the veil of heaven to God.

There is judgment here. This is not anti-Semitic—remember that the writer and a large part of his original audience were Jews—but an announcement that the old ways and the old religious establishment are on their way out. This was apparently the interpretation of the Jewish leaders themselves. Both Josephus and the later rabbis wrote that, around A.D. 30, the destruction of the temple was foreshadowed when the sanctuary *opened of its own accord* (Josephus, *Jewish Wars* 6:293–94; Talmud, *b. Yoma* 39a). These

23

sources do not mention the curtain, but the timing and interpretation of the portent are enough to suggest that they are referring to the same event.

In the Gospel account, it is significant that a Roman centurion is the first one to "get it." Even if his understanding of the title *Son of God* derives from the hero myths of his culture, this is a start, a sign that God's Spirit will soon be given to all people, not just the Jews. By the time Mark's Gospel is written, decades later in Rome, its audience will include many soldiers who risk their own crucifixion by identifying themselves as followers of Jesus. Whatever their views of temples and judgment, what a fresh wind it must have been to bring them the news that one of their own, some swarthy career soldier with blood on his hands—*this* blood—provides the first commentary on the pivotal event in human history.

Mysteries of Womb and Tomb

The beginnings and endings of the Gospels involve angels coming down or the risen Jesus returning up to heaven, but they don't make reference to the sky opening. Here the barriers to be penetrated are the virgin womb of Mary and the stone-sealed tomb of Jesus. What is amazing is that these very objects are connected by language and tradition to the veil of the sky and the temple curtain. The connections are hidden beneath the surface—probably deeper than the writers themselves were aware—in the language and traditions of the Jews.

Consider first the story of the Annunciation, when Mary is told that she will give birth to the Messiah (Luke 1:26–38). There is a long history of association between female genitalia, virginity, and architectural chambers and barriers. To *enter a woman's tent* was a common euphemism in the Old Testament for sexual intercourse, and God himself is said to *open* the wombs of Leah and Rachel (Gen. 29:31, 30:22). To the rabbis, an *open door* is a euphemism for lack of virginity, and in one place the open sky and plowed earth are likened to *the female that opens for the male.* The rabbis referred to female genitalia in architectural terms, with the vagina, significantly, termed the *vestibule.* In several places, the vagina is referred to as the *house of love.* The Song of Solomon contains numerous double entendres, including *a garden locked is my sister* (4:12), *I would bring you . . . into the chamber of the one that bore me* (8:2), and *if she is a wall . . . but if she is a door* (8:9). In the most metaphorically explicit text (5:2–8), the maiden hears her lover cry *open to me,* she is undressed, he puts his *hand* through her *door,* and she *opens* to her beloved.

There are some remarkable parallels to the story of Mary in a work of historical fiction written by an unknown Jewish author around the time of Jesus. In *Joseph and Asenath,* the heroine is a beautiful Egyptian virgin, and the author spares us no symbolic detail of her abode high in an impregnable tower surrounded by a gated and walled garden filled with fruit trees. Asenath sees the hero Joseph from her window, her mother introduces them, but as a righteous Jew he rejects her as an idol worshiper. Somehow nonetheless impressed by Joseph's charm, Asenath retreats to her chamber, fills her *window curtain* with ashes, and begins a long repentance. Suddenly, she looks out the window to see the sky rent, and an angel enters her chamber from heaven, tells her not to be afraid, commends her righteousness, and promises her numerous blessings, including Joseph. Eventually, following her conversion to Judaism, she gets her man, and they live happily ever after.

25

Luke's account of the annunciation to Mary presents some obvious parallels. Gabriel, the angel visitor, is sent from God and *enters in to* the house of Mary, whose virginity is simply stated, not embellished by images of guarded gardens. God's favor is announced, Mary is told not to fear, and immediately blessing is promised. But in this case, the proclamation focuses not on Mary but on the identity and role of Jesus: Gabriel affirms both at the beginning and end of his message that the child born will be the Son of God (1:32, 35). And as in the sky-rending scenes, it is God's Spirit who makes all this happen: *The Holy Spirit will come upon you* (1:35). The pattern is the same. A physical barrier—in this case, Mary's virgin womb—is "penetrated" by God. Immediately a heavenly message, with some reference to the activity God's Spirit, reveals the significance of Jesus.

In the announcement of the resurrection, the object of our interest is the tomb, particularly the sealing stone that formed the barrier at its entrance. The kind of tomb in which Jesus was buried was shaped and described like a house. Such a tomb was commonly carved into a hillside, with a large chamber divided into "rooms" or alcoves where the dead were laid, and a vestibule, the entrance to which was covered by a sealing stone.

The symbolic value of burial stones goes back to early civilizations and continues to the present. Ever notice how carefully most people step around cemetery markers? This habit can be traced to the traditions of ancient civilizations, where stones were placed atop or before grave openings to protect the living by "containing" the soul of the deceased. The sealing stone of a tomb had a similar meaning for the Jews of Jesus' day. According to the rabbis of the time, mourning rites commenced from the closing of the grave with the sealing stone. Contact with this stone, or even the space near it, brought about the same ritual uncleanness as contact with the corpse of the deceased. The sealing stone was the symbolic barrier between this world and the next.

The women who come to the grave of Jesus witness this barrier penetrated, the stone rolled away, and a heavenly messenger inside the tomb who tells them of Jesus' resurrection. It is consistent with the pattern we have already observed that the witnesses must enter the tomb to find the messenger. To be inside, with the door signifying the veil between worlds, puts the women on the earthly side of the barrier. The women are essentially looking *up,* because the barrier has been penetrated from below: *He has risen.* In other words, by leaving the tomb through its sealing stone, Jesus moves through the barrier of the sky to heaven. From this point on the appearances of Jesus, including his ascension, are appearances of the risen Lord from heaven.

After the Resurrection

We see the pattern of barrier penetration in several events after the resurrection, including Jesus' sudden appearance on two separate occasions in closed rooms where the disciples are gathered (John 20:19–29). Each time we are told that the doors of the room are shut or locked—clearly to stress the "impenetrability" of the room. Jesus moves "down" from his heavenly state, presenting an intriguing mix of attributes already observed in other passages. Like an angel, he appears mysteriously and reassures his terrified audience. He takes the authority of God himself in bestowing the Holy Spirit on the disciples, sending them out to be his representatives and to forgive the sins of others. Still, he is quite human, as he demonstrates by showing his recent wounds. The response to all of this, ironically, comes from the once-doubting disciple Thomas, who proclaims *My Lord and My God!*

Special mention should be made here of an earlier event in Jesus' career, recorded in three of the Gospels, called the transfiguration. Jesus climbs to the top of a mountain with several of his disciples and suddenly appears in brilliant light, accompanied by Old Testament figures Moses and Elijah. A cloud enshrouds them, and God's voice pronounces, *This is my Son, the Beloved; listen to him* (Mark 9:7). The event is intended as a "preview of coming attractions," giving the disciples an idea of the glory that Jesus will possess following his resurrection. For our purposes, it fits the pattern perfectly if we understand that climbing a mountain is another way to penetrate the barrier of the sky. This is common enough in the Old Testament, from Moses on Mount Sinai to the mountaintop visions of the prophet Ezekiel.

Following several post-resurrection appearances to his disciples, Jesus ascends to heaven from a mountaintop (Acts 1:6–12). Again, the presence of God is indicated by a cloud, into which Jesus disappears as he is taken up into heaven. Angels appear and pronounce that the event foreshadows Jesus' second coming. This serves a double purpose, informing the disciples that Jesus will not continue to appear to them as he has and letting them know that when he does return, it will be as the figure of power and judgment foretold by Scripture and by Jesus himself. In so many words, the heavenly messengers say what every messenger has said following a barrier penetration scene: *this is the Son of God.*

Stepping Back to View the Pattern

I have jumped all around four Gospels to show the pattern of barriers penetrated followed immediately by announcements concerning Jesus' true identity. Viewed from the back of the tapestry, this is like pointing to threads of the same color, but the view may still be confusing, with these threads moving in several different directions, some long, some short. What is the view from the front?

It is important to appreciate that the Gospels were originally written not as a quartet but as independent documents. Each combines original and shared material, each stresses particular themes, each was written for a different audience with distinct needs. The pattern of barrier penetration followed by announcement occurs in each, with differences reflecting the individual character of each Gospel.

Mark's Gospel contains three barrier penetration stories: the baptism and crucifixion, marked like boundaries by the graphic verb of ripping for the sky, with the mountaintop transfiguration of Jesus resting like a fulcrum in the middle of the story. Matthew and Luke include the transfiguration, but they add material about Jesus' birth and the events following his resurrection—in effect widening the borders of the tapestry. John's Gospel includes much new material, sharing with the other Gospels only one penetration story (Jesus' baptism) and similar details in the resurrection account, but adding other material, including the appearances of the risen Jesus in the locked room.

If we combine the patterned elements in the four Gospels, a vivid picture emerges. Imagine the letter W partially submerged in water. Viewed from water level, a diagonal line leads from top left down into the water, up and out once, then under again, and finally, top right, out again. Now imagine that it is not a water line but the divide between the heavenly and earthly realms or dimensions. Here is a diagram of the movement of God in and out of the world in the person of Jesus, heralded by similar announcements at every important transition: Jesus' conception, baptism, transfiguration, death, and resurrection. It is a movement or pattern of remarkable balance and symmetry.

With the exception of Mark's deliberate choice to use an unusual and graphic verb for ripping at the beginning and end of his Gospel, it is unlikely that the Gospel writers planned or were even aware of this symmetry, nor is it likely that they were even aware of the connections in language and tradition between important symbolic barriers. There is a level of appreciation we must reserve for the Author behind the authors.

Birth and death are mysteries, and in between we live beneath the sky for a while in our frail little dwellings. We enter life through the door of a woman's womb, we enter God's presence through the door of a house of worship, we enter eternity through the door of a tomb. People like the pioneer psychologist Jung have helped us to understand the connections between these basic elements of our existence, and it should not surprise us to see the ultimate story told in such fundamental terms. God the lover penetrates our world, passing through the vestibule and curtain of Mary's womb and through the veil of the sky to walk with us. In death, he passes back through the curtain of the temple and the sealing stone of the tomb and once again through the veil of the sky. With the opening of every door he tells us who it is who comes and goes and will come again. He is the author of the drama, the weaver of the tapestry. And wonder of wonders, God incites and invites the players, each one of billions of tiny threads, both to see and to be God's art.

3

the man who would be god

ONCE UPON A TIME THERE WAS A LITTLE BOY WHO WAS
told that he would be a god when he grew up, or maybe
sooner. As things turned out, it was sooner. When he was
seventeen, his father died and he acquired the world, a pack-
age deal that at the time included divinity. So he murdered
his little brother and his mother, turned over the busywork
to some old politicians, and got on with the business of
playing god. The time was A.D. 54. The place was Rome.
The boy's name was Nero.

To make things a bit easier, there was already a mecha-
nism in place, a sort of divinity game whose rules were
understood by the people of Rome. It seems that, even then,
everyone loved a parade. A Roman parade was known as a
triumph. This traditional procession had evolved from
ancient Etruscan and Greek ceremonies calling for an
appearance of Dionysus, the dying and rising god, whose
part was played by the king. The Romans substituted
Jupiter for the older gods, made each successive triumph
more lavish, and finally replaced victorious generals with
the emperor, who transformed the ceremony into a display
of his own divinity. All of this was done while retaining cer-

31

tain traditional elements to remind the audience of its heritage—and perhaps to lend a bit of much-needed credibility to the notion of a seventeen-year-old god.

We can reconstruct the traditional elements of a triumph by studying the writings and monuments that have survived. Travel in time with me, consider a detailed account of a Roman triumph, and imagine, if you will, that you are a resident of Rome in the mid-first century, a subject of the man who would be a god, and perhaps a follower of the God who would be a man. As such, you would know the story quoted in the following pages from Mark 15:16–39.

> Then the soldiers led him into the courtyard of the palace (that is, the praetorium); and they called together the whole cohort.

The elite troops of the emperor were known as the praetorian guard, and their headquarters in Rome were known as the praetorium. These were the men whose allegiances made or broke emperors, and they were always called together *en masse* at the beginning of a triumph.

> And they clothed him in a purple cloak; and after twisting some thorns into a crown, they put it on him.

The emperor, as triumphator in the procession, was always clothed in a ceremonial robe and crown before the parade began. There are indications that in Nero's time, the outfit was kept on a human-sized statue of Jupiter in a temple in central Rome, removed only for the emperor's use in a triumph. The face of the statue was painted bright red, and the emperor wore red face paint during the triumph. Bright red, like blood, to indicate life. The purple robe was a symbol of power: purple dye was rare and expensive, and no one but the highest orders of Roman society were allowed to wear it.

And they began saluting him, "Hail, King of the Jews!" They struck his head with a reed, spat upon him, and knelt down in homage to him. After mocking him, they stripped him of the purple cloak and put his own clothes on him.

As the triumph began, the emperor would appear before the praetorian guard in his ceremonial garb. The soldiers would show their support by formally saluting him and shouting out his titles.

Then they led him out to crucify him.

If you really wanted to make a point, you took some time to make it. It was less than half a mile from the praetorium to the center of Rome, where the culmination of the triumph took place. But in order to increase the drama, the procession occupied the better part of a full day, involving great numbers of soldiers, officials, condemned slaves, captives, bearers of incense, and carriers of placards that proclaimed the titles and accomplishments of the triumphant one. He did not simply "go" but was "led out," sometimes carried along the parade route, known as the *Sacra Via*, in a special chariot or curule chair.

They compelled a passer-by, who was coming in from the country, to carry his cross; it was Simon of Cyrene, the father of Alexander and Rufus.

A key role in the triumph was played by a bull. In order to depict the dying and rising of the god-ruler as realistically as possible, the animal was privileged with a brief but critical role in the play—the death part. In monuments that show the progress of the triumph, the bull is always shown walking alongside the triumphator wearing a crown and ceremonial garments of its own to help the audience identify the bull with the triumphator. And in every monument depiction of a triumph, there walking alongside that bull is an official who carries over his shoulder a cross-shaped, double-bladed axe, the instrument of the victim's death.

> Then they brought Jesus to the place called Golgotha (which means the place of a skull).

Crucifixion was common enough in the Roman world that major cities set aside areas for multiple and prolonged executions. Crucified bodies, some still living, others in various stages of decomposition, would there be displayed as a warning to others. In Rome, the place was called the *Campus Esquilinus,* the "place of vultures." In Jerusalem, it was given a Hebrew name that people in Rome would not understand without a translation: *Golgotha,* "the place of a skull," or more literally, "the place of the (death's) head."

Dionysius of Halicarnassus records the legend that, during the laying of a foundation for a temple on a certain Roman hill, a human head was discovered, and soothsayers proclaimed, "Romans, tell your fellow citizens it is ordered by fate that the place in which you found the head shall be the head of all Italy." According to Dionysius, "since that time the place is called the Capitoline hill from the head that was found there; for the Romans call heads *capita.*"

The temple of Jupiter Capitolinus, or more simply the Capitolium, was the destination of every Roman triumph. After the procession wound through the streets to the Forum, the triumphator would ascend to the place of sacrifice, the place named after a death's head.

> And they offered him wine mixed with myrrh; but he did not take it.

The supreme moment of the triumph was the moment of sacrifice. As numerous monuments of the period depict it, just prior to the sacrifice of the bull, the triumphator was offered a cup of wine, which he would refuse and then pour on the altar or on the bull itself. (Highly-expensive myrrh added to wine was not a sedative but a symbol of the value of the sacrifice.) The wine signified the precious blood of the victim, and this critical moment of the ceremony linked triumphator, wine, and victim, as did the similar garb worn by the emperor and the bull. In other words, the bull was the god who died and appeared as the victor in the person of the triumphator. All of this was shorthand for a long process of ritual development familiar and acceptable to people living at the time.

> And they crucified him, and divided his clothes among them, casting lots to decided what each should take. It was nine o'clock in the morning when they crucified him.

Immediately after the wine, the sacrifice. At that moment, the bull died, the emperor lived, the god died, the god lived. Resplendent in his robe and crown, Nero was exalted above the people.

> The inscription of the charge against him read, "The King of the Jews." And with him they crucified two bandits, one on his right and one on his left.

Although the focus of the triumph was Nero, he was not alone on stage. Again and again, in both written and monument depictions, he presents himself before the people accompanied by two others, one on his right and one on his left. This was done not only in Rome but throughout the ancient world, and in fact the tradition survives in American politics, when the Vice President and Speaker of the House appear on either side and just below the level of the President as he addresses Congress. This threefold arrangement continues an ancient tradition. It is a symbol of solidarity, a message that the two men who could pose a serious threat to the power of the triumphator are in fact united in his support. Roman emperors like Nero employed their leading generals for this purpose.

> Those who passed by derided him, shaking their heads and saying, "Aha! You would destroy the temple and build it in three days, save yourself, and come down from the cross!" In the same way the chief priests, along with the scribes, were also mocking him among themselves and saying, "He saved others; he cannot save himself. Let the Messiah, the King of Israel, come down from the cross now, so that we may see and believe." Those who were crucified with him also taunted him.

And so the emperor received the willing praise of his people, from the gathered population to the officials of his reign, even from his leading generals. What an occasion, to appear before the people as a god!

> Now when the centurion, who stood facing him, saw that in this way he breathed his last, he said, "Truly this man was God's Son."

The culmination of all this for Nero was not merely a roar of approval from the crowd. It involved a particular statement from the people of Rome, a ceremonial shout at the moment the sacrifice was complete. Then, and only then, Nero could revel in his own divinity, when he heard the sound of their cry: "*Triumpe!* The god appears!"

Postscript

At the same time that all this was taking place in the Forum, there was a man named John Mark visiting Rome.

He was only a Jewish writer passing through, so of course Nero knew nothing of him; but Mark knew about Nero, and so did the friends he was visiting. Nero was very unpopular with the Roman people, particularly with Mark's friends, whom Nero had made scapegoats for a fire in downtown Rome, using many of them for torches and pet food without bothering to kill them first.

Mark and his friends were very confident that, in spite of his ability to sponsor a great parade, Nero was not a god. In fact, they had another candidate. And what was amazing from the perspective of Mark and his friends was how much Nero's triumph was like another story they knew, a story that took place in an obscure corner of the empire where a group of soldiers had once staged a mock triumph to humiliate a prisoner. That prisoner, Mark was convinced, was precisely what Nero pretended to be. He was not a man who would be god, but a God who would be man. It would be a benefit to Mark's Roman friends, who already knew the basics of the story, to write it down in such a way as to highlight the comparison. They would see God's sense of irony. They would see that their own persecution contained a hidden glory, just as it had for their Lord. They would proclaim that, in the words of Mark's friend Paul, "Christ always leads us in triumphal procession, and through us spreads in every place the fragrance that comes from knowing him" (2 Cor. 2:14).

4

god's pyramid scheme

WHEN I WAS A SOPHOMORE IN COLLEGE, I HAD A DISTANT crush on a very distant woman named Jennie Winston. She was tall and blond and athletic, and rumor had it she had recently won a beauty pageant. Since she was so beautiful, I deduced that she must also be highly intelligent and sensitive and thoughtful and charming. The trick now was to meet her. We had some mutual friends, but she was a year ahead of me in school, and I figured she was probably dating a brain surgeon named Lance who played in tennis tournaments and drove a Porsche. Jennie always seemed to be smiling, but her eyes never focused on anyone, least of all me. I have learned from living in Southern California that celebrities never look at anyone directly because eye contact invites unwelcome conversation. But how was I supposed to know that as a nineteen-year-old Midwestern college student, hoping to bask in the glowing light of Jennie Winston's countenance?

Then there came a fateful afternoon in February when, returning to my dormitory, I spotted her a hundred yards away, walking toward me. Alone. I had just enough time to go through the options. Vocal tone is so important. I could try the confident baritone, "Hey, Jennie, how ya doin'?" Then there was the warm, sensitive, higher-pitched,

"Hi Jennie, isn't it just a great day to be alive?" Or maybe I would catch her off guard with a suave, "Hi, Julie—oh, I'm sorry, is it Joanie?" Any of these approaches might start a conversation, and who knows where that might lead? While I was considering these options, the distance had closed between us, and it was important that I begin to observe the universal sidewalk etiquette, which is to avoid looking directly at oncoming pedestrians until they are a few feet away.

And so it was that as Jennie approached, I pretended to look at some nearby trees, awaiting the critical moment that would determine the course of history. Did I mention, by the way, that this was the Midwest? In that part of the world, hostile winters sometimes cause sidewalks to crack and buckle. Occasionally one concrete slab sticks up just a tiny little bit more than the one next to it. Not enough to notice, really, especially if you are looking at some nearby trees.

Where was I? Oh, yes, about ten feet from Jennie Winston. And at that moment—I relive this now in slow motion—as my head swivelled from a polite distance to within the striking range of those lovely blue eyes, just then my shoe encountered one of those sidewalk slabs protruding no more than a quarter of an inch higher than the one next to it, and in less time than takes to say "this relationship just ended," I was sprawled at the feet of Jennie Winston—or rather, where her feet would have been had she not gracefully and silently skirted my prostrate form and continued on to class or lunch or a tennis date with Lance.

Jennie, if you are out there now, middle-aged, a little chubby, wondering why Lance works such long hours at the hospital, I want you to know that my foot is fine, and I caught myself before my face actually hit the cement. I also learned a valuable lesson, but it took me years to fig- ure out because my ego stayed on that sidewalk long after my body picked itself up. What stayed with me was the incredible difference a quarter of an inch can make. How dangerous it is to be *almost* there, *almost* right.

The Stumbling Block

It always struck me as odd that the Jewish religious leaders of Jesus' day were so antagonistic toward him. They read the same Bible, so they knew the prophecies of a coming day when healing and forgiveness would accompany the arrival of the Messiah, literally, "the anointed one," the one upon whom God's Spirit is poured. And there was Jesus, healing, performing miracles, pronouncing forgiveness, receiving a crucial endorsement from his well-known contemporary John the Baptist, and teaching his followers to practice righteousness. Yet the religious leaders attributed Jesus' powers to the devil, accused him of blasphemy, and had him executed by the Romans on a trumped-up charge of treason.

The Jewish sect known as the Pharisees, which gets the most attention in the Gospels, differed with Jesus on many fine points of the law regarding purity, but it seems that there was more to unite them than to divide them. Unlike other sects, the Pharisees used the same Scriptures as did Jesus, believed in an afterlife, and worked diligently at the grassroots level to encourage others to obey God. The Pharisees developed the synagogues (in which Jesus occasionally preached) as community centers of learning, prayer, and worship, they worked constructively with the Romans to preserve Jewish religious autonomy, and they enjoyed a reputation among the people as virtuous and tolerant. The Sadducees, by contrast, were distant from the people, elitist, sticklers for law and order, focused on temple regulation, and collaborated with the Romans. The Zealots were a militant group who eventually incited an ill-fated rebellion against Rome that led to the destruction of Jerusalem and the temple in A.D. 70. The Essenes, not mentioned in the Bible but known from other literature (especially the Dead Sea Scrolls), were a separatist sect obsessed with purity who eventually joined the rebellion against Rome. After the terrible devastation of that war and the loss of the temple, all but one of these sects disappeared. It was the Pharisees who survived, reconstituting Judaism around the observance of the religious law, which they derived from the Bible and their own tradition, passed down by word of mouth through generations of teachers known as rabbis. Eventually their oral tradition found written form in two main documents, the Mishnah (third century) and the Talmud (sixth century). So it is that orthodox Jews today preserve in their writings some traditions that go back to the time of Jesus and earlier. From them we derive some clues about this group that still waits for the Messiah Christians claim has already come.

During the time of Jesus, the most important rabbi in Jerusalem was Gamiliel. When he was not studying the Scriptures or working in the Jewish legislative body known as the Sanhedrin, Gamiliel would teach the best young Jewish minds of his day. One of these up-and-coming Pharisees was Saul, who came to Jerusalem from a distant province to study under the great scholar. After the death of Jesus, Gamiliel counseled members of the Sanhedrin not to be too hard on those who claimed that Jesus was the Messiah and risen from the dead, because *if this plan or this undertaking is of human origin, it will fail; but if it is of God, you will not be able to overthrow them—in that case you may even be found fighting against God!* (Acts 5:38–39). Saul did not agree with his teacher, and we observe him shortly after-

41

wards supervising the stoning for "blasphemy" of a Christian named Stephen. Then, *still breathing threats and murder,* Saul asked the authorities for power to extradite Christians from Damascus to Jerusalem.

The high priest granted Saul the power to persecute, and the rest is history. Saul got *so close* to Damascus, but when he was just outside the city, his horse seems to have encountered one of those sidewalk slabs sticking up just a quarter of an inch, and Saul hit the ground, blinded by a bright light, and then he heard a voice. Next thing we know he has changed his name to Paul and is traveling around the empire, more often than not getting the tar beat out of him by his former fellow Pharisees for preaching that Jesus is the Messiah after all. It was the cross, he wrote later, that had been the problem for him. To the Greeks, he explained, the idea of a crucified God is simply crazy. But to the Jews the cross is something else. Paul calls it a "stumbling block"—something to stub one's toe against.

To appreciate the importance of this expression, we need to step carefully back into the world of Saul the Pharisee, star pupil of the rabbi Gamiliel. From this vantage point, we may begin to see how the death of Jesus can be so close to what people like Saul were waiting for that they could trip over it.

Sin and Forgiveness for One and Many

Humanity has always operated on the religious principle that there is no such thing as a free lunch. A somewhat more technical way to put this is that when things go wrong, or when people do things wrong, a price must be paid. As a way of dealing with spiritual matters, this is a logical extension of relations between people: if you break my fence, accidentally or on purpose, you need to build me a new fence or provide an equivalent compensation. If you rape my wife or kill my son, the cost to you will be enormous, perhaps your very life.

How does this principle connect to God? Beginning with the assumption that God is the creator and, in an ultimate sense, the giver of food and shelter and all good things, people thank God in a symbolic sense by gifts of "life": grain, animals, money, time. When people give "'til it hurts," such a gift is both literally and figuratively a sacrifice. When a person recognizes that God continues to provide life and blessings in spite of that person's failure to live up to the standards of behavior God desires, a sacrifice takes on a slightly different shade of meaning. Now it is a recognition of God's mercy. It is not a question of "buying off" God, because forgiveness is already in place, as evidenced by the continuing blessings of food, shelter, family life, and peace. If those things fail, well, it is no more than we deserve. So in worship and sacrifice we are not accomplishing justice, we are expressing gratitude for God's mercy. At least that's the way we should look at it, but it is easy enough to fall into the notion of an angry God who is going to nail us for our sins if we don't constantly "feed" him in various ways. It is also easy to develop a critical spirit toward others who don't seem to be holding up their end of the bargain with God. These tendencies appear to have been the spiritual downfall of Jesus' opponents, but as he made clear, this wasn't the fault of the system but of their abusive attitudes.

The "system," or what Jews of the time called simply *the law*, involved a logical progression of sacrifice or cost in accordance with the severity of a person's wrongdoing. Essentially, there were four levels. At the lowest level, there were sins of neglect or omission, things that should have been done but were not done. For such "light" sins, animals were given to

43

the temple priests for sacrifice, and these private offerings had to be accompanied by repentance; that is, one needed to be sorry for wrongdoing and committed to obedience in the future. Repentance alone was enough, but a sacrifice was considered a meaningful outward expression of a changed heart.

At the next level were sins of transgression, things that were done that should not have been done. These kinds of sin were dealt with by repentance and the annual Day of Atonement, or *Yom Kippur*. The central event on the Day of Atonement was the sacrifice of one goat and the sending into the wilderness of another goat, which symbolized God's forgiveness and removal of sin from his people.

There were some sins so "heavy" that neither personal repentance nor the Day of Atonement were enough. Personal suffering, inflicted by religious authorities or directly by God (e.g. disease, loss of loved ones), had to occur when the sins in question were as serious as heresy or blatant disobedience.

The most serious offense of all was abuse of the name of God. This seems odd to us in an age when "Oh my God" is a common expression, and the use of God's name in anger is considered "cussing" in the same sense as "four letter words." In bad taste, perhaps, but hardly deserving of a jail term, much less capital punishment. And yet for the Jews of Jesus' day, the name of God was so directly connected to his holiness that even to speak the name was considered a crime punishable by stoning to death. But even this penalty was a door to salvation, and so the repentant offender was instructed to say, just before execution, *May my death be an expiation for all my sins.*

Up to this point we have considered only sins and different levels of suffering or sacrifice that signified atonement for individuals. In the personal offerings and in the national Day of Atonement, animals paid the price for human wrongdoing, so there was some idea of a price paid for others, but the prevailing notion was that you took care of your own business and nobody else could do it for you. There were, however, some interesting exceptions to this.

In several places, the rabbis wrote about a value accruing to others when a righteous man or sage died. To show honor to such a person by grieving is a kind of sacrifice in that the survivor willingly suffers because this good person is gone. The rabbis wrote, *If one sheds tears for a holy man, the Holy One, blessed be He, counts them and lays them up in His treasure house.*

Even more effective than the death of a righteous man is the death of a child. *According to the rabbis, when there are righteous men in the generation, the righteous are seized* [by death] *for the* [sins of the] *generation; when there are no righteous in a generation, school-children are seized for the generation. And in another place, we are told that if a man busies himself in the study of the* [law] *and in acts of charity and* [nonetheless] *buries his children, all his sins are forgiven him.* It is not difficult to understand how the death of a child can be a greater sacrifice than the death of a righteous man. There is no worse pain for a parent than to lose a child. The feelings of unfairness, helplessness, and loss of future—both the child's and the parent's—are overwhelming. The sacrifice is even more pure than that of a righteous man, because a child has had no opportunity to commit serious sins, and certainly has done nothing remotely deserving of the ultimate punishment of death.

What could have a greater effect than the death of a righteous man or the death of a child? Only one event: the death of a martyr. One who died for the faith was usually depicted as unusually righteous and certainly courageous. A martyr not only died but was subjected to terrible tortures and a shameful form of death at the hands of godless persecutors. And perhaps most importantly, a martyr was understood to represent all of God's people. Unlike a righteous man, whose death affected his friends; or a child, whose death affected a single family, one who died for the faith in effect died for all Jews. A document written about the time of Jesus records the last prayer of a Jewish martyr from the second century B.C.: *Be merciful to your people and let our punishment be a satisfaction on their behalf. Make my blood their purification and take away my life as a ransom for theirs.* The author later comments about this man and his fellows, who endured terrible suffering at the hands of their pagan tormentors: *Through the blood of these righteous ones and through the propitiation of their death the divine providence rescued Israel.*

Do you see the logic of this progression? On the individual level, the more serious the wrongdoing, the more severe the requirement of sacrifice or suffering, up to the point of death. And when it comes to death, the more righteous or innocent the sufferer, and the more terrible the suffering, the greater the effect.

There are two planes or lines here moving inexorably toward one another: the quality of the sacrifice and the degree of harm. If only there could be a *perfectly* innocent sufferer, dying the *most horrible* of deaths imaginable. Would the planes meet at the top? Would the result of that meeting be a perfection of atonement, an effect both complete and permanent? Would it be God's pyramid, a rock to endure forever—or a stumbling block?

The Shame of the Cross

In terms of the quality of sacrifice, the New Testament makes it clear that Jesus was not only innocent of the charge

46

of treason that got him killed, he was in fact sinless. His innocence gives his sacrifice a power infinitely superior to that of the temple sacrifices: *For it was fitting that we should have such a high priest, holy, blameless, undefiled, separated from sinners, and exalted above the heavens. Unlike the other high priests, he has no need to offer sacrifices day after day, first for his own sins, and then for those of the people; this he did once for all when he offered himself* (Heb. 7:26–27). Because he was innocent, this phrase "once for all" means not only once for all *people* but once for all *time.* This is basic Christian doctrine, but it may be news that it so neatly completes the "hierarchy of atonement" understood by the Pharisees. Remember, though, that there is another element or plane that contributes to this completion, and that has to do with the severity of punishment. To understand this we must take a long, unpleasant look at death by crucifixion.

The cross has become a piece of jewelry, a beautiful decoration in a church, a symbol of faith. It is difficult for us to pass back through centuries of tradition to see crucifixion as a form of capital punishment so horrible that polite people would not so much as mention it. Comparison to more recent forms of execution—the electric chair, the firing squad, the guillotine—are inadequate because these methods attempt to end life in a relatively quick and painless manner, whereas crucifixion was designed for precisely the opposite reasons: it was intended to make death as slow, agonizing, and humiliating as possible.

The actual crucifixion of a prisoner was only the culmination of a series of tortures, some of which are recorded in the Gospels. To begin, the victim was usually beaten and then flogged with a scourge. The Roman scourge was not a horse whip but a multi-thonged arrangement about three feet long with bits of lead sewn into the cords, so that after a few strokes, the flesh would open, sometimes to the bone.

This would be enough to kill some prisoners who were already weakened by imprisonment and rough treatment.

After torture, the victim was paraded through the streets to the place of execution, often carrying a sign announcing his crimes and the horizontal beam to which he would later be tied or nailed. The place of crucifixion would be in a central place easily observed by the local populace. According to the historian Quintillian, *Whenever we crucify the guilty, the most crowded roads are chosen, where the most people can see and be moved by this fear. For penalties relate not so much to retribution as to their exemplary effect.*

At the place of crucifixion, the victim was hoisted up on a vertical beam permanently fixed in the ground. There he was left to die, a process that could take several days. Some victims died from exposure or from the effects of previous torture, but technically, crucifixion accomplished death by slow strangulation. As the victim's legs and arms weakened, the bones of the shoulders gradually closed in on the throat, cutting off the breath. This is why, in the case of Jesus and the two criminals who were crucified with him, soldiers came to break their legs: without the ability to hold themselves up, strangulation would occur quickly. The usual Roman method was to leave the body on the cross to rot, but either out of consideration for Jewish customs or because special permission was granted in this case, the body of Jesus was removed for burial.

The punishment of crucifixion was reserved for the worst of criminals, slaves, and people found guilty of treason. A normal citizen committing a capital crime was beheaded— a comparatively quick and honorable death. In polite society, the cross was an obscenity. According to the famous orator Cicero, *The very word cross should be far removed not only from the person of a Roman citizen but from his thoughts, his eyes and his ears. For it is not only the actual occurrence of these things or the endurance of them, but liability to them, their expectation, indeed the very mention of them, that is unworthy of a Roman citizen and a free man.*

So revolting was the concept of crucifixion to first-century audiences that the word rarely occurs in Roman literature, and when it does, it is often in plays involving the crude speech of slaves. In these sources, the cross is called variously *the tree of shame, the criminal wood,* and *the infamous stake.* At Pompeii one line of graffiti reads, *May you be nailed to the cross.* Thus crucifixion became an insult, a word of cursing, and there was even an accompanying hand signal. To give someone the sign of the cross in the first century had precisely the opposite purpose that it would have today.

If the idea of crucifixion was abhorrent to decent people in the ancient world, imagine the difficulty of trying to convince them that a god—indeed, *the* God—had willingly endured such a punishment. There is an interesting passage in a play by Aristophanes, *The Frogs,* where two travelers in the underworld dispute over which is a god and which is his slave. One suggests concerning his companion, *You should flog him well, for if he is a god he won't feel it. Whichever of us two you first behold flinching or crying out—he's not the god.* In the world of the New Testament, a god couldn't even feel pain, let alone die, and to suggest that a god would volunteer for this—that was simply preposterous. So Paul writes that the Cross is *folly to the Gentiles.* It was laughable, a major public relations problem for the early Christians. In fact, they did not commonly use the cross as a symbol until several hundred years later.

For Jews, there was insult added to injury. Crucifixion was a punishment by and for Gentiles, unlike stoning, which was the prescribed form of capital punishment under Jewish law. Crucifixion involved public nakedness, which was a particular insult to a modest people like the Jews. The prisoner was paraded through the streets on the way to the place of execution, increasing his shame and inviting abuse from observers. And in most cases the victim was not buried—an additional insult to the Jews, who treated their dead with great honor and ceremony. In fact, the Pharisees believed that exposure of the corpse after death was a form of suffering that had atoning value for the deceased. For Jews, then, crucifixion was both a horror and a dishonor, the worst possible death.

God's Pyramid Scheme

So it is that the planes meet, the most innocent victim possible experiences the worst form of suffering that could be inflicted, especially on a Jew. According to the New Testament, the result of that meeting is the perfection of atonement, an effect that applies to everyone forever. This is God's finished work, a pyramid, a rock to endure. And yet Paul, a scholar of his religious tradition, a man trained to follow the pattern of these developments to their logical and wonderful culmination in Jesus, calls the cross *a stumbling block to the Jews.* Why didn't they get it?

They were on the right path, but they were looking at the trees, thinking about something they wanted far more than I wanted Jennie Winston, and they didn't see it coming, that little crack in the pavement. How did it happen?

Many of the Old Testament prophecies describe what Christians now believe will happen at the second coming of Jesus, a radical breaking into history on the part of God when he makes everything right and establishes his righteous rule directly on a transformed earth. There isn't much there about suffering, especially on the part of the promised Messiah. The martyr of Psalm 22 and the suffering servant of Isaiah 53 were understood as referring to Jesus by the early Christians (and by Jesus himself), but the rabbis interpreted these as references to the suffering of the nation. In the first century, they were suffering the humiliation of occupation by a foreign power with no respect for their beliefs. They were looking for a Messiah who would come down the sidewalk toward them to deliver them. Nor were they entirely political about it. They were diligent about personal righteousness, desiring earnestly to honor God by their actions and to persuade as many of their fellow Jews as possible to realize the ideal of a godly community. It is natural that they would expect their Messiah to honor their religious laws in detail, and their Scriptures did not prepare them to expect a Messiah who would challenge their definition of righteousness, much less claim equality with God.

I will take this a step further. I believe that if we could go back in time and set up a formal debate between Jesus and a leading Pharisee of the day like Gamiliel or his student Saul, using the tools of interpretation that we would use today to interpret the relevant documents, *the Pharisee would win*. And that is precisely my point—and I think, I believe, I hope, the point of Jesus. Being right—having the best arguments, compiling the most evidence, even living in exemplary consistency with one's beliefs—does not always make a person right. There are still going to be those pesky little cracks in the sidewalk, and it makes all the difference to see them, or to respond in a certain way after failing to see them and falling on one's face. That way is the way of humility, the choice to find the little surprises as I go and adjust my steps or to laugh at myself and learn rather than curse the crack that trips me. Sidewalks are good things, made by good people. But the little cracks are made by God.

5

jesus goes to therapy

THE FOLLOWING IS AN IMAGINARY TRANSCRIPT OF A
conversation between Jesus (J) and a modern psychologist
(P—or if you like a name, Dr. Peterson).

*P: Jesus, since you are a new client, I'm interested to know why
you came today and how you feel about being here. By the
way, is it okay if I call you Jesus—or do you prefer Messiah,
Lord, Christ, or some other title?*

J: Jesus is just all right with me.

P: Oh I get it, like the rock song!

J: Yes, I like that one better than Handel.

P: You mean you listen to human music?

J: Oh, yes, all kinds. People produce all the music in heaven.
I'm partial to reggae these days, but country seems to be
taking over, especially since the apostles persuaded
Mozart to do some crossover work.

P: *Well, that's very interesting, but of course we're here to talk about you, so let's get back to that, shall we?*

J: Fine. Is there any particular place you want to start?

P: *I have a feeling that with you, I can skip the small talk and get right to the substantive issues. For example, it is important for each of us to understand our own childhood and the traumas that we carry with us all our lives. Suppose we start there.*

J: Well, my childhood was pretty idyllic, and not all that eventful, as you can see from the Gospels, which skip right past those years to my early adulthood.

P: *But we can't afford to skip over them here. So tell me: wouldn't it be obvious to your family and friends that there was a perfect individual in their midst?*

J: No. Despite what you see in films, I didn't have light hair, a white robe, or an English accent. My very Semitic nose ran when I caught a cold, and I did not miraculously stretch boards when I cut them too short in Joseph's shop.

P: *But if you never did anything wrong, wouldn't that be rather obvious?*

J: Not in a village of farmers and tradesmen. To such people the heart and its motives are secrets. We did not have words for such things. I was one of many obedient boys.

P: *What of your family, though? Didn't they notice how unusual you were and talk about it with others?*

J: My parents were simple and quiet people. They chose not to tell others about me, and there was much they did not know. In fact, as time went on with nothing unusual happening, they began to doubt their own memories about the events of my birth. We lived in a village far from the center of things, and our days were filled with long hours of toil.

P: *Then as a young man—just like that—you left home to change the world?*

J: Many young men do. Not all of them get quite as much support from their fathers as I did. Of course, to tell people that your father is the God of the Universe sounded just as crazy then as it would today.

P: *When did you begin to sense confusion and hostility from people, and how did that make you feel?*

J: It wasn't the common people who objected; it was the religious leaders. They wanted to please God by making and following perfect rules. As soon as I began to teach and to heal, they believed that I was breaking their rules and offending God.

P: *And this disapproval and anger from the leaders of your people, how did that make you feel?*

J: I continued to teach and to heal.

P: *Yes, but inside, what was that like for you, desiring to be understood and to make a difference, and so few people noticed, and those who should have appreciated you hated you and plotted against you?*

J: I was a mother, longing for her children. I made food. I was the sea, longing for the shore. I made waves.

P: *Yes, in more ways than one. And your opponents had you killed for your efforts. But didn't you have some feelings of confusion or resentment toward God, that he sent you on this mission knowing you'd fail with your people?*

J: I understood that I would prevail by obedience and not by success. I would not make my way by force. I came making peace, providing for the poor, healing the sick. I was to be the lamb of sacrifice. This kind of death is not failure.

P: *But didn't it feel terrible to have to go through all that?*

J: You speak constantly of feeling. My body suffered terribly at the hands of my persecutors, but the hurt *in my heart* was not for the way the people treated me or the way my Father treated me—it was for the pain people chose for themselves.

P: *That's great, Jesus, but I need to challenge you on this, because I'm sensing some denial issues here. Let's keep talking about your relationship with your Father. It looks like God forced you, or at least persuaded you, to suffer for the good of others. Isn't this a form of child abuse and a terrible example? After all, haven't many of your followers hurt others in your name, and then used your example to maintain that suffering is good for them?*

J: I told my followers they would suffer. I also told them it would be unfair. The truth that suffering can be good for a person does not justify the one who causes that suffering. Love *offers* to suffer, it does not *require* suffering from others. Abuse of one's wife or child or enemy is terrible enough, but to do it or defend it in my name is doubly abusive.

P: *Precisely my point! Isn't that what God did in persuading or forcing you to die? And doesn't that make you the original battered child, covering for an abusive parent?*

J: May I ask you a question or two?

P: *Well, I guess, as long as it doesn't get us off track—but it is a little unorthodox.*

J: Good. In my line of work, I don't get much opportunity to be "a little unorthodox." But you raise a very serious issue. When you do the will of another, is it because you obey, or because you agree?

P: *It might be either. It depends.*

J: And do you ever do the will of another without being asked by that person? For example, when you give a holiday surprise to one you love well, how do you know what that person wants?

P: *The more time I spend with someone, the more I care about what makes them happy, and the more likely I am to come up with the perfect gift. There is always a little guesswork, though, because the two of us don't know each other perfectly— but that is part of what makes a holiday surprise so much fun.*

J: Precisely my point. My Father and I were so close that there was no guesswork. I offered the holiday surprise of my death, not as obedience or agreement, but as the outflow of a perfect understanding between me and my Father. The gift is for everyone, and it's a food gift, so you don't have to worry about it being the right size or needing batteries. It requires nothing more, and nothing less, than to eat me.

P: *That sounds like cannibalism. Aren't you concerned about offending people?*

J: I regret that I do not offend more people. Too many eat cute little wafers from silver dishes and forget what the ceremony represents. Too many more make me a relic of history and turn their faces from my living eyes. But there you are with blood on your hands, and here I am in your office, sitting on your couch. What will you do with me?

P: *Yes, there you are on my couch, so to speak. But I must say that I am a little uncomfortable with the personal direction this is heading. It feels at times like you are turning my questions back toward me.*

J: I see. If it weren't for the inconvenient fact that I am the Messiah, you could pass me off as having a real Messiah complex. It always has gotten me in trouble, this habit of reversing expectations—or "confronting avoidance," as you might say. How does it feel to be exposed?

P: *(Long pause) . . . I think we need to get back to my questions. After all, this is your time, not mine.*

J: (Short pause) . . . As you wish.

P: *Was that a "Princess Bride" allusion?*

J: With me, everything is an allusion, nothing is an illusion.

P: *I'll have to think about that one.*

J: Yes, you will.

P: *Pain. I want to get back to pain. There is so much in the world, don't you agree? And do you understand how difficult that makes it for people to believe in a loving God?*

J: Is that a question about me or about you?

P: *I guess it's just a general question about the problem of pain.*

J: Then I cannot answer it.

P: *Why not?*

J: Because there is no "problem of pain."

P: *What do you mean?*

J: The way you put the question, pain becomes a theory, an abstraction. Pain is not experienced as a theory, by "the world" or by "humanity." Last week a woman in Somalia named Batu watched the last of her three children die of starvation. What comfort can I give to the heart of Batu? What hope can I give to her soul? This is the problem of pain that I know, the experience of which and the response to which occurs one person at a time. What pain do you know that is not an abstraction, and can I help you to redeem it?

P: (Long pause) . . . *Once again, with all due respect, I think that we are moving away from my proper role here, and I think I'd like to find some ground between the abstract and the personal.*

J: These two are sand and rock. Do you know of a better place than rock upon which to build?

P: *Maybe we can step away from the building for just a bit and work on the foundations, get back to your story.*

J: As you wish.

P: *Okay, point taken. I confess that I'm beginning to feel like the one being analyzed. So call it escape, or at least room to breathe, but I want very much to ask you more questions about the times you had to struggle with pain and doubt.*

J: What times were those?

P: *I'm thinking of two times. The first was when you struggled in prayer in the garden of Gethsemane, just before your arrest, and the Gospels report that you asked God to "let this cup pass from me." Can you tell me how you were feeling at that moment?*

J: I wanted to find a ram in the bushes.

P: *What do you mean by that?*

J: In the Scriptures, when God saw the obedience of Abraham, who was about to sacrifice his own son, God directed his attention to a ram caught in a nearby thicket, and the cup passed from Abraham. I thought there might be such a way for me to avoid suffering.

P: *Of course. It was natural for you to fear the abuse and pain you were about to experience.*

J: You misunderstand. My prayer was not motivated by fear, but by the wrongness of my death. To the end, I wanted a right way, but there had always been turns along my path that were dark to me until I walked forward. So I concluded my prayer, "yet not what I want but what you want."

P: *That sounds like resignation after a moment of weakness.*

J: That would have been true if there had been two wills involved. As it was, I simply wanted two things at once.

P: *So you were divided within yourself? Confused?*

J: No. To pray is to speak truly what you want, not to calculate what you are going to get and adjust your prayer accordingly. I truly wanted both a way out of the wrongness of my death and a way in to the rightness of my Father's will.

P: *And did you find that?*

J: Yes. The way into the rightness of my Father's will was to die, and the way out of the wrongness of my death was to rise again.

P: *But didn't you know all that in advance, and didn't that take the sting out of it?*

J: The lash still cut my flesh, the nails still pierced me, I was still mocked by those I came to save, I was still abandoned by those who had followed me. Would you ask a woman in the midst of labor how it feels to be a mother?

P: *Good point. Let's move ahead to the climactic moment of pain for you, your famous cry from the cross, "My God, my God, why have you forsaken me?" It surprises me that your followers would record this moment of weakness.*

J: Why? They recorded their own.

P: *Yes, I suppose that was difficult for them, to show themselves as bumbling so much when, by the time the Gospels were written, they were big shots.*

J: They never acted like big shots. That is how they and those who followed them conquered an enormous police state without the use of force. Or even television.

P: *Do I detect a little sarcasm?*

J: Yes. I don't like television, especially around Easter when they show reruns of bad movies about me. Television is only a slightly dumber way than the Crusades and the Inquisition to keep millions of people from paying attention to the truth.

P: *Did you just use the expression "slightly dumber"? I believe that should be "slightly more dumb," and I'm surprised that you could make a grammatical error, much less use sarcasm.*

J: Even divinity is a bit rough around the edges, especially when making a point. You will recall that my nose got really out of joint about the Pharisees and their trivial games with righteousness. That kind of thing still annoys me to no end.

P: *Once again, I'm amazed. But let's get back to what I asked about earlier, your cry from the cross. So much has been written about that, all the speculation about how God could feel abandoned by God and theological complications regarding the doctrine of the Trinity. But I want to know what it was like to feel that terrible anguish of aban-*

donment, and did you really feel the weight of all the world's sin on your shoulders, spiritually speaking?

J: Such words come from the world of the mind, not from my moment of pain.

P: *I don't understand that statement.*

J: When I hung on the cross, I felt the same pain in my body as did other victims of that torture. Because I had been badly beaten earlier in the day, I was already near death when I arrived at the place of execution. The pain and weakness made it difficult for me to speak or to think clearly. I said very little. But that was because I was dying, not because I was imagining and feeling the full meaning of my death.

P: *That goes against what I understand to be historic Christian teaching.*

J: Good. I have little to do with historic Christian teaching. Most of it is an attempt to clarify my teaching in ways that neatly avoid actually following it. Kind of like what you are doing by asking me about my feelings while you hide from your own heart. You would make a fine theologian.

P: *Ouch. But at the risk of another act of avoidance, I can't help but ask: Do you have an axe to grind with theologians?*

J: A spear point, actually. Theologians got me killed and continue to cut me. Truth is like a flower whose beauty is not improved by dissection. Theology is like gold, good in itself but dangerous to own.

P: *So when it comes to denominations and religious disputes, you don't like to take sides?*

J: Behold my side, and the wound there.

P: *I see. Sensitive subject. I'll go back to my earlier question. Are you saying that you didn't feel an enormous weight of sin and abandonment by God when you were crucified?*

J: No. Not in the way you are thinking.

P: *What else can I think about your famous "cry of abandonment"?*

J: Do you remember that I wandered in the wilderness before I began to teach and to heal?

P: *Yes. What has that got to do with it?*

J: From that beginning, my father showed me that I was the nation in one person. I wandered in the desert as they had, but I did not bow to temptation, nor did I rebel. I entered the land as they had, but I brought peace and healing and abundance. In making me the final sacrifice, my father took all the lambs and goats that had died for the people and made the people die instead—but now I was the people, I was the nation in microcosm.

P: *The concept makes sense, and it is consistent with your story—but what does it have to do with how you felt at the moment of your death?*

J: Listen carefully: It was not me as a man who was forsaken at that moment, but me as the nation.

P: *You mean you were that detached even then, so caught up in this theoretical understanding of yourself?*

J: Not detached. Identified. Why do you think I quoted Scripture instead of simply screaming?

P: *I don't know. You tell me.*

J: My cry was from a psalm about abandonment—but not quite all about abandonment. It ends this way: "All the ends of the earth shall remember and turn to the Lord. . . . Future generations will . . . proclaim his deliverance to a people yet unborn." I died there, a nation died, and a greater people was born. My cry signaled both.

P: *If this is true, why didn't people get it?*

J: Some did. Do you remember what happened immediately after my cry?

P: *The temple curtain was torn.*

J: Right. A sign of judgment, as my last breath—the wind of the Spirit—tore through the symbol of the old way. And what happened immediately after that?

P: *That's when the Roman soldier pronounced that you were the Son of God.*

J: Right. A sign of hope that the wind of the Spirit would blow right back in a new way, to fan a flame through all nations.

P: *But what about the theology and your feelings of anguish?*

J: The theology came later, and the concern about my feelings came much later—quite recently, in fact. If imagining my anguish leads you to follow me, I am all for it. But if it only feeds your hunger to experience feelings, you will starve.

P: *Why are you so negative about feelings? And yet you seem equally discouraging when it comes to thinking, at least in terms of theology.*

J: In your day, you see these two as alternatives, and your religion reflects this. You are either holding hands while chanting bad music, or writing books to win meaningless wars of words. There is a third way, and a fourth.

P: *What are they?*

J: The third way is to *imagine,* and what you will create out of your imagining will require that you think well and result in you feeling well. The fourth way is to *act,* which is the simplest and best of all.

P: *Act in what way?*

J: My way. You already knew before you asked, but you want the cup to pass from you.

P: *Yes, well—oh, I see we're just at the end of our time for today. Exactly fifty minutes. This has been great, Jesus. I think we accomplished a lot for a first session. Will you come again?*

J: Oh, yes. You won't want to miss it.

P: *I meant to my office.*

J: I know. I can't resist a good straight line. As for another meeting, I'll decide when you do. Then I'll call.

6

the god in the garden

THE READING IS TAKEN FROM *NEW IMPROVED GENESIS,* chapter one:

In the beginning of modern times, about a hundred years ago, Man looked at his universe, and it seemed without form and void, and darkness was upon the face of the deep, and the spirit of mankind looked over everything, and Man said, "Let there be science." And there was science.

And Man saw the science that he had made, that it was good, and with it he divided all things. He created a science to rule the day, all the things he could see, and he called it Natural Science, even unto Physics, Chemistry, and Biology. And he made a lesser science to rule the night, all the darker things about himself, and he called it Social Science, even unto Psychology, Sociology, and Politics. And Man saw that it was good. And there was morning and evening, and the modern day had begun.

And Man divided all the things he saw: the waters above, the land, the waters below, the grass, the fruit tree yielding fruit, the swarms of living creatures in the waters, the birds that fly above the earth, and moving creatures of every kind that are on the earth, including himself, a higher primate distinguished from the other creatures mainly by his ability to destroy everything. And Man saw that all this dividing and classifying was good, and the destroying was fun too. This all took several evenings and mornings, and that got him up to the fifth day.

And Modern Man said, "T.G.I.F." But then he thought, "Wait a minute. What does the G stand for?"

And then Modern Man said, "Let us make God after our own image, according to our likeness." And so he did. He blessed God, and he said to him, "Be distant and keep to yourself, because we have already filled the earth and subdued it and classified it, and there really isn't a whole lot of room left for you, but you certainly are a pleasant thought."

And then Modern Man planted a garden, and there he put the God he had formed. And he called the garden Safe Respectable Religion. And out of the ground of that garden, Man made to grow trees that are pleasant to the sight, and flowers, and he put a fine building in the midst of the garden, because good landscaping enhances property values. And the Lord Man took God and put God in the building and said, "God, enjoy yourself, but whatever you do, stay in the building, for in the day that you leave it you shall surely die."

Then the Lord Man said, "It is not good for God to be awake; someone might wander into the building and find him and be frightened." So the Lord Man caused a deep sleep to fall upon the God he had made, and he slept. And Man laid him in a box inside the building and put a lid on the box and laid a curtain over it and placed tall candlesticks on top of it, so he could come there from time to time to remember the God he had made. Then Modern Man said,

At last, I have expressed fully the mystery of life
And the depth of my mind;
I shall call this God Personal,
For out of my personality he was taken.

And there was evening and morning, the sixth day, and Modern Man saw that it was very good, because all this was done leaving one extra day in the weekend for golf.

So ends the reading for the day. I suppose if we had an equivalent hymnbook we could now turn to #372, "How Great We Art." Modern culture and religion deserve all the parody we give them, but we have to be careful not to let our critique rest with those "out there." Those who are "out there" are not listening, so the noises we make about human rebellion and decline merely bounce off the walls we have made to keep ourselves as "in here." If there is a reason to point a finger, it is that the finger points at us, each of us, because each of us has this tendency to make up God as we go along.

Most of us are willing enough to say that God created us, but we often live as though we create God. I don't mean in the secular materialist sense of declaring that God is a projection of wishes and superstitions. Few people can be that sure of God's nonexistence. We'd rather give him the benefit of our doubt, but that is just the problem. Most of our time is occupied by problems we can get our minds around: finish this project at work, prepare dinner, pay the phone bill by the tenth. It is natural to shelve the problems we can't get our minds around: God is present but I don't feel anything, God answers prayers but not always yes, God changes lives but my worst habits remain. Expressions like "get our minds around" and "shelve" imply that in our souls there are spaces and ways to divide those spaces, so we speak of ourselves in architectural terms: "I don't have room for this in my life right now," "You are putting up a wall," "That wasn't in her comfort zone."

Where does God fit? The reality we need to get by from hour to hour, to work and eat and pay bills, is a pretty small place—the smaller and more well-defined the better. Someone as big and uncertain as God is outside. Not far outside because, again, we give him the benefit of the doubt. We assign him a place nearby, a place we can go when the time or need arise. A place of convenience. A *nice* place, like a garden. "I come to the garden alone, while the dew is still on the roses," says one sentimental old hymn, "And he walks with me, and he talks with me, and he tells me I am his own." And then what? I leave the garden and go back to my house—the real, practical, physical space of my life—and God never follows. How convenient. What is the alternative? It is terribly threatening to imagine that God might not respect my boundaries; that God might, without my invitation or without my knowledge, pass through my walls, demand more from me, do more with me, than I am willing to allow.

Admit it. How much more attractive would God be if he were the God in the garden, if we could keep him in a place of our own imaginative creation, where he walks around quietly blessing flowers and bunnies and small children. We could let him out, or let ourselves in, when we want a hug, when we are grieved or depressed or guilty or frightened. But those aren't constant needs, of course. The real world is investment portfolios and kids who need rides to practice and a new movie to see and a vacation to plan. Most of this world we have created is not a place for God. Keep him inside the garden wall, inside his box.

What if he doesn't want to stay there? What if one day he refuses to stay in a box? Let's suppose he did, and let's suppose we call that day Easter.

A long time after the story of the first garden, the Garden of Eden, there was a story of another garden and Jesus, who didn't fit into the world people of his time had created for God, so they killed him and put him in a box in a garden and put a lid on it.

This is part of what happened afterward, from the Gospel of John, chapters 19 and 20:

Now there was a garden in the place where he was cruci-fied, and in the garden there was a new tomb in which no one had ever been laid. And . . . they laid Jesus there.

Early on the first day of the week, while it was still dark, Mary Magdalene came to the tomb and saw that the stone had been removed from the tomb. So she ran and went to Simon Peter and the other disciple . . .

[The disciples came, investigated the empty tomb, and returned to their homes. They weren't quite sure what had happened. We pick up the story with the woman who stayed behind.] *Mary stood weeping outside the tomb. As she wept, she bent over to look into the tomb; and she saw two angels in white, sitting where the body of Jesus had been lying, one at the head and the other at the feet. They said to her, "Woman, why are you weeping?" She said to them, "They have taken away my Lord, and I do not know where they have laid him." When she had said this, she turned around and saw Jesus standing there, but she did not know that it was Jesus. Jesus said to her, "Woman, why are you weeping? Whom are you looking for?" Supposing him to be the gar-dener, she said to him, "Sir, if you have carried him away, tell me where you have laid him, and I will take him away." Jesus said to her, "Mary!" She turned and said to him in Hebrew, "Rabbouni!" (which means Teacher). Jesus said to her, "Do not hold on to me, because I have not yet ascended to the Father. But go to my brothers and say to them, "I am ascending to my Father and your Father, to my God and your God." Mary Magdalene went and announced to the disci-ples, "I have seen the Lord," and she told them that he had said these things to her.*

There is a curious and important detail in this story that really is the main point. Mary didn't recognize the risen

Jesus until he called her by her name. When God comes out of the box, out of the garden, when he decides to defy our expectations, to break out of our limitations, he does it in the most intimate manner possible, and he follows up with a frightening demand.

Back in chapter 10 of John, when Jesus was beginning to explain this, he said something similar. *The good shepherd,* he said, *calls his own sheep . . . and the sheep follow him because they know his voice* (John 10:3–4). Now, the risen, glorified Christ calls one sheep, Mary, by name and commissions her—a mere woman in a time when the word of a woman wasn't worth much, a former prostitute in a culture where one's past was unforgivable. This woman he calls by name and commissions to be the first witness of the greatest event in history.

A chapter later the theme is driven home again, when Jesus shows up at the beach and talks to gutless enthusiast Peter. Again, Jesus calls him by name and then gives him a task.

"Simon, son of John, do you love me more than these?" He *said to him, "Yes, Lord; you know that I love you." Jesus said to him, "Feed my lambs."* And then Jesus repeats this two more times. Why the threefold repetition? A few days before, in the garden, three times Jesus asked Peter and his disciples to stay up and pray with him, but they chose sleep. It was only a garden, after all, and sleep was much more convenient. But later that night Peter denied Jesus three times. And now, three times: Do you love me? Do you love me? Do you love me? Do you get the point? Do you get the point? Do you get the point? This God comes out of the garden and knows how to get personal.

What if it's true? What if he refuses to stay put, declines to remain a common, garden-variety God, is not content to remain on the pages of a book? If it is true that he rose from the grave, then maybe he rises now from our confining notions, even from the letters of this page, and demands to be recognized and followed.

The sheep hear his voice. He calls his own sheep by name and leads them out. When he has brought them out, he goes ahead of them, and the sheep follow him because they know his voice. He won't stay in the comfort of the sheepfold, and he won't leave the sheep there either. Just when you thought it was a safe little chapter in a book, he strikes you with the reality that he knows you, he knows your name, and he wants you for something.

What kind of God did you come to this chapter to find, anyway? What Jesus have you planted for yourself in the garden?

Imagine yourself Easter morning in a garden, like Mary, alone with your thoughts, weeping inside about something that should be there and it isn't. We all have some pain, some terrible pain, some very personal pain. Let me imagine what words might tell of yours.

"I am confused. I thought direction in life would be more clear by this time. I thought I'd know what I'm good at and others would appreciate me and there would be a clear path to the future. Instead there is just this big empty road with no signs on it and maybe a few people are cheering for me but I'm still not sure where I'm heading."

"I am lonely. People have let me down. People die, people change, people leave, people stay but don't have time for me or don't notice how badly I need them. People don't notice me, or they stop noticing me. I thought life would be more like a Norman Rockwell painting, a whimsical hometown place where comfortable folks drop by and family is near and dear. It turns out life is more like a modern abstract, the kind you walk up to and ask nervously, 'What is it?'"

"I am busy. Life won't slow down, and I can't seem to slow down. There is always another crisis at work or at home, and when there is a breathing space I just want to put my feet up. I can't think about anything important, much less figure it out, in the few fleeting moments I have to myself. Life seems to get more complex and frightening."

"I am guilty. I've done things I regret, but I'm afraid to make amends, and I'm not even sure how to try. I hold most of it inside myself, because I would only repulse people if they knew what I really am inside. My bad habits are ingrained, and my good ones are easy to fall out of. Even to begin to do more good would feel hypocritical to me. I don't want to get used to myself being this way, but neither do I have the power to change."

Where is God in all of this? Where do you go to find him? Where are the answers? Not in a garden with some sentimental stained glass image of God we have created for our convenience. That Jesus isn't big enough, powerful enough, to deal with the hurt and confusion of real people.

But if Easter is true, the glorious and maybe frightening news is that Jesus is not in his garden grave. He's alive. He is standing behind you while you sit in that chair reading these words or while you sit in the office or in front of the television or behind the wheel. He is speaking your name, calling you, whispering something about peace and following and that something's got to give . . . to give . . . to give. You can't see him, and you can't hear him, maybe because he is so much larger and louder than your physical senses can comprehend.

This is only a chapter in a book, and it is almost ended. Then what? Most likely you will leave this quiet place of contemplation, this garden, for another activity. Tend the children, fix a meal, pay some bills. That's life too. But in the quiet moments punctuating all the hubbub, remember that you did not leave this place alone. Jesus will not stay buried for you here any more than for Mary. You are being followed.

And everywhere that Mary went the Lamb was sure to go.

7

return of the living dead

I HAVE ALWAYS BEEN FASCINATED BY THOSE POLICE sketches that reconstruct suspects from the recollections of witnesses. On several occasions I have tried the method on large groups of Christians, asking them to picture in their mind the apostle Paul and then by show of hands tell me what he looks like. The conversation goes like this:

Is he tall or short? Short. Everybody was short in the first century.

Do you picture a well-fed man or a thin, rather wiry sort? Thin and wiry (almost unanimous).

Is he bald or does he have a full head of hair? Here I get a pretty even split, but since far less than half of men are bald, we'll have to give Paul the shiny nod.

How about facial hair? Is he bearded or smooth-shaven? About sixty/forty in favor of a beard. So we'll give him a trim one.

Do you picture him in his thirties, forties, fifties, or older? Most people put him in his mid- to late fifties.

A few more questions reveal that Paul is dark-haired, dark-complected, and has a prominent nose. Now, since we're trying for something more than a mug shot, something like a portrait, I ask a few more questions.

How do you picture the expression on his face? Does he appear relaxed or intense? Smiling or stern? About an eighty/twenty split in favor of an intense, stern expression. Paul is not a fun guy, apparently.

Now picture Paul's whole person, his body language, his activity. Do you imagine him sitting at a writing desk, preaching to a crowd, talking with another person, alone pacing back and forth in thought? It may be that the details of the facial portrait influence the answer here, but almost everyone imagines Paul alone, and a large majority picture him pacing back and forth.

What emerges from this sketch is an almost stereotypical Type A personality. Brow furrowed, project-oriented, aggressive, powerful, organized, the kind of person who today might be an attorney or a corporate executive. You see him in airports, walking briskly, carrying a new leather briefcase, loudly dictating instructions by cell phone to some quaking underling.

Of course we do not know what Paul or any biblical character looked like. What we imagine is based on the assumption, fair or not, that a person's appearance tends to be consistent with his personality. Paul almost certainly was short, dark-haired, and dark-complected—as was every other Jewish character in the New Testament story. Most people can accept this until they are asked to imagine Jesus looking like Woody Allen or Mary looking like Dr. Ruth Westheimer. For them, we want something a bit more northern European. But Paul can keep the rabbi look because, although he exchanged a star of David for a cross, essentially he was the same soldier with a new general.

At least that's what many of us seem to think, if my police sketch work is any indication. Paul is the intense one, the intellectual, the arguer, the manager. We need people like him to get the job done, but we'd rather not have him over for a Sunday afternoon barbecue, and we'd just as soon have our daughter marry some guy who is going to be around on weekends for Little League games.

My purpose now is to undo everything I have just written. I am not sure I can transform Paul into a fair-haired, well-fed uncle with laugh lines around his twinkling eyes, but I am confident that a closer look at his life will modify the caricature of the apostle as Project Manager, New Religion Division.

Paul's "Quiet Years"

According to Paul's own account and the partial record of his career in the New Testament book of Acts, he was converted to Christianity by a supernatural encounter with the risen Jesus. This happened while he was on his way to Damascus to round up Christians for punishment as heretics—which they were from the orthodox Jewish perspective of Paul's preconversion life. After this dramatic experience, rather than hanging around Jerusalem as a kind of apprentice apostle, Paul started to work immediately as an evangelist in distant parts, including three years in Arabia and ten years in Cilicia, his area of origin, which corresponds to southeastern Turkey today. We have very little information about this period. If Paul wrote letters, none survive. The book of Acts focuses on the last decade of his life as he travels through what is now western Turkey and Greece, founding churches and writing the letters that comprise about one third of the New Testament.

It is from these letters that we get a glimpse back toward Paul's earlier career and an important insight into the development of his character. Some time around A.D. 55, toward the end of one of his longer letters, Paul offers some autobiographical information about his past. Among other things, he recounts that he has experienced *imprisonments, with countless beatings, and often near death. Five times I have received at the hands of the Jews the forty lashes less one. Three times I have been beaten with rods; once I was stoned. Three times I have been shipwrecked; a night and a day I have been adrift at sea* . . . (2 Cor. 11:23–25).

What this flashback reveals is, quite literally, a glance at Paul's back.

The thirty-nine lashes (so numbered to provide a margin of error on the maximum forty lashes prescribed by Scripture) were a synagogue punishment for heretical teaching. Such a punishment could be deadly. Although the leather strips were not weighted with lead or bone like the Roman scourge, the repeated blows on the back would eventually open the skin, and the possibility of infection was as dangerous as the trauma of the beating itself.

A beating with rods was a secular punishment, and this too proved fatal to many victims. Presumably in Paul's case the torture was administered for disturbing the peace, since civil unrest was an occasional result of his new ideas, which threatened established religions. Usually Paul was simply run out of town, since his Roman citizenship (probably in Paul's case a privilege of birth into a prominent family) offered some protection from violence. But on a few occasions, Paul either chose not to identify himself as a person with such status or the local authorities considered beating a respectful alternative to execution.

Stoning was the Jewish form of capital punishment, in Paul's case probably for blasphemy by association with Jesus. This was not done as films depict, with an angry crowd pelting baseball-sized rocks from twenty feet away. Rather, the victim was crushed by having dropped on his chest a single rock heavy enough that two people were required to lift it. If he still showed signs of life, the same rock was dropped again or more large rocks were thrown by others from close range. For Paul to live through such a punishment was either miraculous or would have appeared so to those who came to retrieve his body (Acts 14:19). His survival must still have involved severe physical trauma, broken bones, and a lengthy recovery.

The point of describing all this is to remove any supposition that Paul was some kind of traveling lecturer, an ivory-tower type who sat around thinking up doctrines to put in letters. I lived in the ivory tower for twelve years, and for all the whining we did about college politics, I don't recall anyone having scars—although there was always the danger of a paper cut from a carelessly handled memo. This was not Paul's life.

Imagine the scene, with Paul tried and convicted for the third or fourth or fifth time in a synagogue trial for trying to convince his fellow Jews that Jesus is the Messiah. The authorities return a sentence of heresy, remove Paul's cloak, then pull his tunic down to expose his back. There they would find a statement written in scars that would speak as powerfully as any words that Paul might speak. Here is a man who is beyond theological disputes, a man who will not be deterred by the threat of horrible pain and death. Here is a man who, for all intents and purposes, cannot be killed because he has already died.

The Return of the Living Dead

A close look at Paul's back makes sensible and powerful some of the statements he makes about the effect of Jesus' death on his life. It is not merely doctrinal reflection, but scar tissue that enables Paul to write that *while we live, we are*

79

always being given up to death for Jesus' sake, so that the life of Jesus may be made visible in our mortal flesh (2 Cor. 4:11). In another place he explains, *I have been crucified with Christ; and it is no longer I who live, but it is Christ who lives in me. And the life I now live in the flesh I live by faith in the Son of God, who loved me and gave himself for me* (Gal. 2:19–20).

And what difference does it make? How is this man transformed by these many near-death experiences, by literally incorporating (taking into his body) the death of Jesus? Not merely by becoming courageous. Paul is freed not only to die, but also to live in love.

I do not know from experience, of course, but my best guess is that it is a lot easier to die for a cause than to live for one. The martyr experiences a moment or maybe an hour of terrible pain, and then it's all over but the heavenly reward and, for those left behind, the legend-making. The near-martyr—or in Paul's case, the *multiple* near-martyr— must reflect on the implications for life of coming so close to death. It may well be that Paul was closer to that Type A stereotype when his spiritual journey began on the road to Damascus, but it is evident that so many trips back from the door of death transformed him inwardly and made him a spiritual life-giver to others.

Vision or Disillusion?

Paul's early years of work as an evangelist on his home turf appear to have had little impact, but things went better on his first missionary journey to western Asia Minor (modern Turkey), and it must have been with great excitement that he embarked on his first "European tour" about A.D. 52 following a visionary experience in which a man pleaded with him to *"come over to Macedonia and help us"* (Acts 16:9–10).

The reality was not so exciting, at least at the beginning. Paul, with a small entourage of coworkers, leaves Asia for the first time and lands at the port town of Neapolis in Macedonia (northern Greece). The next day he journeys inland to the city of Philippi, where a few people are converted to the new faith. But some locals perceive that Paul is a threat to their pagan beliefs, and they persuade a mob and the authorities that he is dangerous. Paul is beaten severely, jailed, then run out of town. He moves west to Thessalonica, where a riot occurs (this time at the instigation of Jewish opponents), and Paul is run out of town again. The same thing happens in Beroea. Paul and his helpers move south to Athens, where he is essentially laughed out of town by educated skeptics. The European Tour isn't going well. No one is coming to the concerts or buying the T-shirts, and if Paul and his friends push much further south, they will be in the Mediterranean Sea.

In Pursuit of the Corinthians

But finally, in Corinth of all places—a port city famous for its decadence—Paul is well-received. A community of believers forms, and Paul remains for over a year building up the people in the new faith.

Eventually, after further travels, Paul finds himself in Ephesus, directly east across the Aegean Sea from Corinth, and there he learns that the Corinthian Christians have turned against him, following new leaders with great charisma who challenge Paul's authority and introduce destructive notions that they claim come from the origi-

81

nal apostles in Jerusalem. Paul immediately sails across the Aegean Sea, but the Corinthians rebuff him, and he returns to Ephesus. Like many a rejected lover, he hopes that a letter will succeed where his personal plea failed, and he sends a written appeal in the hands of his associate Titus. He is so distraught from worry about the Corinthians that he cannot do his normal work of preaching and teaching in Asia. But now it is winter and too stormy to sail, so he travels overland, hoping to locate Titus somewhere in Macedonia (northern Greece). To his great relief, he finds Titus and receives the news that the Corinthians have relented.

Now Paul has them exactly where he wants them, right? This is his opportunity to make them grovel, to patronize them, or at least to "take the high road" by lightly passing over the wrong they have done to him. What he does instead is nothing short of amazing, a demonstration of pure empathy.

Knowing now the historical background of this paragraph, read carefully Paul's words.

> Blessed be the God and Father of our Lord Jesus Christ, the Father of mercies and God of all comfort, who comforts us in all our affliction, so that we may be able to comfort those who are in any affliction, with the comfort with which we ourselves are comforted by God. For as we share abundantly in Christ's sufferings, so through Christ we share abundantly in comfort too. . . . If we are comforted, it is for your comfort, which you experience when you patiently endure the same sufferings that we suffer. Our hope for you is unshaken; for we know that as you share in our sufferings, you will also share in our comfort.
>
> For we do not want you to be ignorant, brethren, of the affliction we experienced in Asia; for we were so utterly, unbearably crushed that we despaired of life itself. Why, we felt that we had received the sentence of death; but that was

to make us rely not on ourselves but on God who raises the dead; he delivered us from so deadly a peril, and he will deliver us; on him we have set our hope that he will deliver us again. You also must help us by prayer, so that many will give thanks on our behalf for the blessing granted us in answer to many prayers (2 Cor. 1:3–11 RSV).

If you were counting, that was nine occurrences of the word *comfort* in the first four sentences, and seven occurrences of *affliction* or its synonyms in the passage. What is remarkable about these words in such concentration and contrast is that Paul is using them to raise the Corinthians' guilt over what they had done to Paul to the level of Paul's physical suffering for the faith and emotional suffering on their behalf. Far from rubbing their noses in their wrong, he portrays their shame as a form of pain from which he longs for their deliverance. Far from forgetting his own past persecution of believers, and far from being embittered by the continuing opposition of legalists, he portrays the situation as a struggle between suffering and comfort, the comfort purchased by the suffering of Jesus. But Paul goes even one step further. In the closing sentence, he tells the Corinthians that he depends on their prayers, that his very work as an apostle is linked to their willingness to plead with God on his behalf.

This is astounding to me. In my own life, on those rare occasions when I am wronged and the other person apologizes, I may not rub it in and lord it over the other, but neither am I likely to lower myself or raise the other. Paul does both, and the distance between his position as a sufferer and the Corinthians' position as wrongdoers is far greater than any distance in my own experience. He shows by these words that he understands suffering and comfort because he has deeply suffered and has been deeply comforted. His return from the brink of death has placed him

83

on the cutting edge of life, in that place where suffering can find meaning. This has become so much a part of his experience that he can write, *In my flesh I am completing what is lacking in Christ's afflictions for the sake of his body, that is, the church* (Col. 1:24). Or later in this second letter, We are *always carrying in the body the death of Jesus, so that the life of Jesus may also be made visible in our bodies* (2 Cor. 4:10).

So it is. Another paradox of the death of Jesus, that to identify with him in his loss is to begin, in this life, to gain all things. So Paul can write truthfully, *For his sake I have suffered the loss of all things, and I regard them as rubbish, in order that I may gain Christ* (Phil. 3:8).

The Artist's Composition

Paul's features were molded, or remolded, not in a cool, quiet study but in the intense heat of persecution and in the long weather of experience. When creating our own composite sketch of this man, we should look carefully at the craft of another Artist. Yes, Paul was a teacher, a thinker, an organizer, an intense, driven personality. But the power of his message was in the love that he learned as he returned so many times from death to life. In this he discovered the link between himself and a living Jesus who in dying had demonstrated perfect love. As a result, Paul's life was given to the people who moved in and out of his life as he journeyed around the Mediterranean world caring for them.

What kind of man was he? After making peace with the Corinthians, Paul stayed with them for several months, during which time he wrote his best known letter, to the Christians in Rome. Two thousand years later, the greatest New Testament scholars sit in ivory towers writing books about the highly-developed, profound theology contained in Paul's Epistle to the Romans. Most scholars join most readers in passing over Paul's postscript to this letter, which contains personal greetings to no less than twenty-six individuals. Paul had never been to Rome.

8

on death and power and one old lady

I WAS A COLLEGE STUDENT WHEN I MET MABEL. IT WAS Mother's Day, and I was taking some flowers to the county convalescent home to brighten the day for some lonely mothers and grandmothers.

This state-run convalescent hospital is not a pleasant place. It is large, understaffed, and overfilled with senile and helpless people who are waiting to die. On the brightest of days it seems dark inside, and it smells of sickness and stale urine. I went there once or twice a week for four years, but I never wanted to go there, and I always left with a sense of relief. It is not the kind of place one gets used to.

On this particular day I was walking in a hallway that I had not visited before, looking in vain for a few people who appeared sufficiently alert to receive a flower and a few words of encouragement. This hallway seemed to contain some of the worst cases, strapped onto carts or into wheelchairs and looking completely helpless.

As I neared the end of the hallway, I saw an old woman strapped up in a wheelchair. Her face was a horror. The empty stare and white pupils of her eyes told me that she was blind. The large hearing aid over one ear told me that she was almost deaf. One side of her face was being eaten by cancer. There was a discolored and running sore covering part of one cheek, and it had pushed her nose to one side, dropped one eye, and distorted her jaw so that what should have been the corner of her mouth was the bottom of her mouth. As a consequence, she drooled constantly. I was told later that when new aids arrived, the supervisors would send them to feed this woman, thinking that if they could stand this sight they could stand anything in the building. I also learned later that this woman was eighty-nine years old and that she had been here, bedridden, blind, nearly deaf, and alone, for twenty-five years. This was Mabel.

I don't know why I spoke to her—she looked less likely to respond than most of the people I saw in that hallway. But I put a flower in her hand and said, "Here is a flower for you. Happy Mother's Day." She held the perfect flower up to her distorted face and tried to smell it. Then she spoke. And much to my surprise, her words, although somewhat garbled because of her deformity, were obviously the product of a clear mind. She said, "Thank you. It's lovely. But can I give it to someone else? I can't see it, you know, I'm blind."

I said, "Of course," and I pushed her in the chair back down the hallway to a place where I thought I could find some alert patients. I found one, and I stopped the chair. Before I could speak, Mabel held out the flower and said, "Here. This is from Jesus."

That was when it began to dawn on me that this was not an ordinary human being. We distributed the rest of my little supply of flowers in the same manner, and I wheeled her back to her room. There I began to learn more. She had grown up on a small farm that she managed with only her mother until her mother died, and then she managed the farm alone. Her social life was limited to the country church near her home, where she had played the piano from the time she was a girl. Finally blindness and sickness and poverty sent her to the county convalescent hospital. For twenty-five years she got weaker and weaker, with constant headaches, backaches, and stomach aches. Then the cancer came. There was little medical care for people like Mabel, people with no money who were merely waiting to die. For company she had three roommates, human vegetables who screamed occasionally but never spoke intelligibly. They often soiled their bedclothes, and because the hospital was under-staffed, especially on Sundays when I usually visited, the stench was overpowering.

Mabel and I became friends, and I went to see her once or twice a week for the next three years. Her first words to me were usually an offer of hard candy from a tissue box she kept near her bed. Some days I would read to her from her beloved Bible, and often when I would pause she would continue reciting the passage from memory, word for word. On other days I would take a book of hymns and sing with her, and she would know all the words of the old songs. For Mabel, these were not merely exercises in memory. She would often stop in mid-hymn and make a brief comment about lyrics she considered particularly relevant to her own situation. I never heard her speak of loneliness or pain except in the stress she placed on certain lines in certain hymns. Once, for exam-ple, while singing "What a Friend We Have in Jesus," fol-lowing the line, "Is there trouble anywhere?" she mur-mured softly, "Oh, yes, there is."

It was not many weeks before I turned from a sense that I was being helpful to a sense of wonder, and I would go to her with a pen and paper to write down things she would say. I have a few of those notes now (I wish I had had the foresight to collect a book full of them), and what follows is the story behind one scrap of paper.

During a hectic week of final exams I was frustrated because my mind seemed to be pulled in ten directions at once by all of the things I had to think about. The question occurred to me, "What does Mabel have to think about— hour after hour, day after day, week after week, not even able to know if it is day or night?" So I went to her and asked, "Mabel, what do you think about when you lie here?"

And she said, "I think about my Jesus."

I sat there and thought for a moment about the difficulty, for me, of thinking about Jesus for even five minutes, and I asked, "*What* do you think about Jesus?" She replied slowly and deliberately as I wrote, so slowly that I was able to write it all down. This is what she said:

"I think about how good he's been to me. He's been awfully good to me in my life, you know. . . . I'm one of those kind who's mostly satisfied. . . . Lots of folks wouldn't care much for what I think. Lots of folks would think I'm kind of old-fashioned. But I don't care. I'd rather have Jesus. He's all the world to me."

And then Mabel began to sing an old hymn:

Jesus is all the world to me,
My life, my joy, my all.
He is my strength from day to day,
Without him I would fall.
When I am sad, to him I go,
No other one can cheer me so.
When I am sad, he makes me glad.
He's my friend.

This is not fiction. Incredible as it may seem, a human being really lived like this. I know. I knew her. I watched her for three years. *How could she do it?* Seconds ticked and minutes crawled, and so did days and weeks and months and years of pain without human company and without an explanation of why it was all happening—and she lay there and sang hymns. *How could she do it?*

The answer, I think, is that Mabel had something that you and I don't have much of. She had power. Lying there in that bed, unable to move, unable to see, unable to hear, unable to talk to anyone, she had incredible power.

What is power? The term gets thrown around a lot these days. We don power suits and eat power breakfasts, we empower others, we work for the powerless, we address the power struggles of gender and race. The word occurs in the Bible, of course, but the sense is almost ironic given contemporary usage.

Not that contemporary usage has changed much since the time of Jesus. Christians in the first-century Greek port city of Corinth, for example, were apparently social climbers who found it a bit embarrassing to have the death of Jesus—and such a humiliating death at that—play a central role in their faith. It appears that, for them, the Christian faith was all about having a dynamic personality, or even supernatural gifts like the ability to prophesy or speak in tongues. It doesn't take much to imagine them sponsoring seminars on directing small groups or on "servant-leadership," with Jesus as the role model. Think of all the good you could do in a position of influence, armed with the name and character traits and powers of Jesus.

Paul writes a letter to these people and pulls the thick executive rug out from under them on the first page. He uses the word *power* a half-dozen times, but every time he connects the word to the death of Jesus, knowing full well what the world thinks about such things. *For the message about the cross is foolishness to those who are perishing, but to us who are being saved it is the power of God* (1 Cor. 1:18).

Paul contrasts this "foolishness" to the "wisdom" of that culture, which exalted sophistication, personal strength, success, and a commanding presence. Not exactly a profile of Mabel. *For God's foolishness is wiser than human wisdom, and God's weakness is stronger than human strength* (1 Cor. 1:25). The idea appears to be that God takes this power or energy released by the death of Jesus and uses it to change people.

Elsewhere Paul describes the change, the application of this power to the individual. It does not entail influence over others but the ability to understand and do what is good. In other words, it is not about doing a few great things but a lot of little good things. This seems simple enough until I think about it in relation to one of my persistent bad habits, or in relation to loving the persistently unlovable people in my life, or to Mabel's persistent joy in the face of such suffering. Then the power required is beyond me. Precisely.

In Ephesians 3:14–21, Paul writes about the energy required for people to love others to such an extent and under such circumstances that are now, at their present level of energy, unthinkable and therefore unaskable. And so he refers to *him who by the power at work within us is able to accomplish abundantly far more than all we can ask or imagine.* Similarly, in Colossians 1:11–12, he describes his prayer that *you be made strong with all the strength that comes from his glorious power, and may you be prepared to endure everything with patience, while joyfully giving thanks to the Father.* The point is that in Paul's mind, as in his life and as in Mabel's life, the power that he has in view does not generate unusual *production* so much as unusual *persistence.*

This is difficult for us to comprehend, because the world operates with a different definition of power. Power is the force required to dominate—people, events, inanimate

91

objects, or money—and often for good ends, for worthy causes. Indeed, we tend to equate the word *power* with those in places of political or intellectual influence.

But for twenty-five years, while the world's leaders calculated how much force of persuasion or arms or economics would be required to make life what it should be, there in that bed was what life should be. There was power. But nobody asked Mabel.

And for twenty-five years, while scholars and their students argued and wrote and wondered about whether there can be a loving God who would create a world in which there is so much pain, there in that bed was pain. And there was that loving God in all his unthinkable, unaskable power. But nobody asked Mabel.

Well, you might ask, was this woman really filled with God's power or just a simple-minded country bumpkin with nothing better to do than sing hymns? I'll let you answer that question for yourself by conducting a little experiment. The next time you have a headache and a stomach ache, maybe a little touch of the flu, go to bed, close your eyes, and cover your ears with your hands, pressing occasionally to increase the discomfort, and don't move at all. Then for an hour, try to do only what Paul recommends in Ephesians 3:18–19, *to comprehend . . . what is the breadth and length and height and depth, and to know the love of Christ that surpasses knowledge, so that you may be filled with all the fullness of God.* How long do you think you could do this with sincerity? Ten minutes? An entire hour? In twenty-five years, there are approximately 170,000 waking hours. How much power would it require to do that for all of that time? And from whom would the power have to come? Mabel didn't know much, but she did know that what matters most matters every minute. And minutes turn into hours.

I read these words I have written, and my eyes fill with tears now all these years later. They are tears not for Mabel but for me, knowing how I have squandered so many of my hours and wondering whether even now I can learn from her. I also wonder whether I can find the words to convey who she was, what she knew. I wonder if she was too far beyond any of us, lying in that bed, for us to understand or even believe in such greatness, much less appropriate any of that power for ourselves.

But you want to, and so do I. How to begin? The first step, I believe, is to recognize the simple but revolutionary truth that such a life as Mabel lived is an altogether new life, not merely some kind of "energy supplement."

Some sense of this is conveyed by Alexandr Solzhenitsyn in *The Gulag Archipelago,* his first-hand account of life in the Soviet political prison system. Solzhenitsyn writes about staying alive and sane in the midst of terrible physical and emotional suffering. At one point he describes the most difficult time of all—the interrogation:

> So what is the answer? How can you stand your ground when you are weak and sensitive to pain, when people you love are still alive, when you are unprepared?
>
> What do you need to make you stronger than your interrogator and the whole trap?
>
> From the moment you go to prison you must put your cozy past firmly behind you. At the very threshold, you must say to yourself: "My life is over, a little early to be sure, but there's nothing to be done about it. I shall never return to freedom. I am condemned to die—now or a little later. But later on, in truth, it will be even harder, and so the sooner the better. I no longer have any property whatsoever. For me those I love have died, and for them I have died. From today on, my body is useless and alien to me. Only my spirit and my conscience remain precious and important to me.

Confronted by such a prisoner, the interrogator will tremble.

I read these words and ask, *Does my interrogator tremble?* He goes by different names: greed, lust, pride, anger, laziness. How long can I hold out against this interrogation, this inexorable power within me working against the good, this enemy who will never let up? Ten minutes? An hour? Twenty-five years? Solzhenitsyn makes the point clearly enough: a life of power demands no less than the sacrifice of that life. The point was made a long time ago by Jesus in words that may have lost some of their punch by repetition without demonstration: *For those who want to save their life will lose it, and those who lose their life for my sake, and for the sake of the gospel, will save it* (Mark 8:35). It is an all-or-nothing proposition.

But what is this "all" in "all-or-nothing"? What does it mean in practical terms to *lose my life?* What force can lift my life out of the reach of my interrogators? What can I do to acquire that kind of power? The beginning of the answer is disturbingly simple: Ask for it.

There are some statements in the Bible that may appear too good to be true, but they are certainly worth checking up on. One of the more simple and common promises is that God will give us good things if we ask for them. *Ask, and it will be given you,* says Jesus. He goes on to explain that you don't give rocks to your children when they ask for bread, so *how much more will your Father in heaven give good things to those who ask him* (Matt. 7:7–11). There can be little doubt that the power to choose and to do good is among those "good things" to ask for.

But I have already asked, and I wasn't suddenly transformed into a saint ready to lay in a sickbed for several decades singing hymns. Maybe I did better for an hour or a day, but I didn't change much or for long. So what are the options? Either God isn't there, or he is there but doesn't keep his promises, or they aren't his promises but the wishful thinking of biblical writers, or I was insincere in asking, or he gives but in little doses. In the following paragraphs I'll consider these options one by one.

Maybe God isn't there. Maybe he doesn't exist or doesn't operate anything like the Christian tradition says he does, caring and involved in the details of my life. Maybe we are just very clever creatures inventing God and religion to give ourselves hope, to keep the dark away. Maybe. But I'm going to give up on attempting to persuade you otherwise even before I begin. There may be a place to discuss proofs and plausibility and philosophical defenses, but this book isn't one of them. After twenty years of theological and philosophical inquiry I can save you a lot of time by promising that an honest appraisal of the arguments will bring you full circle to a choice between viable alternatives. I'll say only that I choose to go on believing, even though at times I feel like the woman in the Bible who could do no more than grab for the fringe of Jesus' robe as he walked by. She was superstitious at best, but she got healed.

Another way of accounting for my asking and not getting is that God doesn't keep his promises. Christians work hard to avoid admitting this. I have never been persuaded by the explanation for unanswered prayer that claims, "God always answers, it's just that sometimes the answer is *No*." Nice try. This strikes me as a perfect example of a parent giving rocks to a child who asks for bread. If we hadn't been *told* to ask for bread, if we had been told that asking is more like a game of "which hand?" that might be another matter. But I learned a great theological lesson the day I told my daughter I'd do anything to persuade her to pull that awful tooth that had been dangling from her gum for two weeks, even take her to Disneyland, and thirty seconds later when she held out the tooth and asked when are we going and I said I had been kidding, well, I can assure you, I lost the ensuing debate in less time than that which transpired between promise and tooth extraction, and I can assure you God would lose the argument even quicker, because he wouldn't waste time as I did trying to save face. No, a loving father doesn't try to pull a fast one on his child and then explain that it is for her own good. Kids aren't stupid, and parents learn either to qualify themselves clearly up front, or find the rocks they substituted for bread someday come back aimed at their heads.

If God does not qualify himself when he tells us to ask for good things and then tells us exactly what those good things are, perhaps we should consider the possibility of a misunderstanding stemming from the "human element" in the message. Could it be that biblical writers got a little carried away, put words in God's mouth, and got God into all kinds of trouble ever since with those who have been applying words to the Bible like *inspired* and *authoritative?* If this is the case, I must adopt a pick-and-choose approach to parts of the Bible that don't seem to square with experience, and I don't know when to stop. Does *Jesus* square with experience? Does humility? Gentleness? Truth? The logical end in that direction is to transform God himself from one who reveals himself in the Bible to a cosmic *It* that biblical writers were lucky enough to glimpse now and then through the tiny windows of their culture. But how did the windows get there? Maybe the universal light just happened to shine out on Mabel through a cross-shaped hole chipped through the wall, and maybe those bumbling disciples were awfully good with chisels, give or take a few wishful promises. Maybe it's all relative after all; maybe we make God up as we go along to help ourselves face the void.

And maybe there is a fable somewhere about a snake that mistook his tail for a mouse and swallowed himself. If not, there should be. Of this I am very confident: a cosmic *It* would not last five minutes in Mabel's room.

Another option I must consider is that my asking for power is insincere. This seems to be an introspective way of playing the "which hand?" game, with the bonus of guilt to add to powerlessness. So Grandma died because my prayer for healing lacked faith, and I sinned because I didn't really mean it when I asked for power to fight temptation. So how do I know when I mean it? When things turn out well. How convenient. Certainly all of our prayers involve a mix of motives, interruptions for daydreams, confusion about what to pray for, expressions of passionate feeling, half-awake mumbling, forgetting important things we should pray about, vain repetition, and occasionally somewhere in there, sincerity. How could we ever gauge the worthiness of our prayers in relation to results? And do we really imagine that God is watching some kind of electronic graph to see if the blips reach high enough on the sincerity meter to qualify for response on his part? I suspect that the sincerity question has a lot more to do with modern navel-gazing than with asking and getting from God.

Maybe God answers my request for power, but he only gives the power in small doses. Genies have a rule, you know, that one of the three wishes can't be a wish for an endless number of wishes. Just be glad you found that bottle at all and don't try to get tricky. Maybe God works like that, imposing a quantity limit on our "good things," giving us only enough power to meet our immediate needs. *This day* our daily bread—not more than we can digest, not enough to hoard, not so much that we forget by tomorrow our need and the one who meets it. After all, the child in Jesus' illustration asks only for bread or a fish, not a grocery store. And we should receive as children, trusting God to act like a sensible father. To modernize the point, what father, if his daughter asks for a new dress, will turn her loose in Saks Fifth Avenue with his Visa card? Ask, but as a child asks; God will give, but as a wise father gives carefully and constructively to his children.

This approach accounts for a lot of my confusion and impatience over the things I ask for and don't get, and it gives credit where credit is due for the good God has done to me and through me over the years. Mabel was not made into a powerful woman overnight, nor was she made powerful in answer to any single prayer. The kind of bread she needed for that was *daily* bread, like the *manna* that came down from heaven for the children of Israel when they wandered in the wilderness, bread that they had to go out together each morning to gather for the coming day, bread that wouldn't keep for even one night. Now, Jesus makes the extraordinary claim that *I am the living bread that comes down from heaven. Whoever eats of this bread will live forever; and the bread that I will give for the life of the world is my flesh* (John 6:51). *Eat my flesh and drink my blood,* he goes on to say, and the narrator reports that these remarks were so offensive that even some of Jesus' followers left him, partly because he sounds like a suicidal cannibal, partly because he makes his own death and our participation in it the key to life. God save us from communion bread disguised by silver platters and lace doilies. We eat raw chunks of him, together, or we each die alone. The words of Jesus and the thoughts behind them are too grisly and too deep and too unsafe for a disciple to invent. Jesus clearly thought that people could only thrive in this life if they joined together continually for this relentless absorption of *him,* piece by piece. Mabel thought so too.

By offering this "little dose" option and tying it in to life in community, I imply that the acquisition of power is a process and that it is only possible with other people around to learn from and to be accountable to. I know nothing about Mabel's mother or her country church except the result. It may be almost impossible today to find a place where such simple, strong belief is nurtured in a tight-knit community of good, hard-working people. It may be that I can be grateful for Mabel's sake, but for me it is only nostalgia. And if I learned of such a place, even something that seemed to approach it, I would be afraid to go there and spoil it, for I am not simple, strong in my beliefs, good, or hard-working. I'd rather get power the new-fashioned way, from a web site.

Is there any hope for me, a post-Mabel man?

I think so. I keep asking, however feebly, for power equal to the obvious tasks of daily obedience and for tasks equal to the not-so-obvious power that may in fact be at my disposal, and I keep dreaming. How do I move from dreaming to doing?

Some years ago I read a biography of Isaac Newton, a dreamer and a doer. There have been few people in history who have demonstrated such power of mind and action. By 1664 he had mastered all the mathematical works written up to that time. In 1665 he became the first to compute the area of the hyperbola, found the method of approximating series and the rule for reducing any dignity of any binomial into such a series, and discovered calculus. In 1666 he was the first to explain the phenomena of color, and he began the modern science of optics. In the spring of that year he began to develop the theory of gravity and to plot the orbit of the moon, leading eventually to his calculation of the orbits of the entire solar system and some of the comets. All of this was accomplished with instruments of his own design and construction. Later in 1666 Newton graduated from college. He was twenty-three years old.

Many years later, an admirer asked Newton how he was able to explain and discover and do so many amazing things. His answer: "By always thinking upon them."

I had to look up Newton's list of accomplishments again to write that last paragraph, but his explanation for them has remained with me like an image burned on my retina. Clearly, such power cannot be a hobby for a person's spare time. It must be an obsession. I turn the thought to a question that has haunted me for many years. *On what am I always thinking?* My daydreams are my life dreams. They are the measure of my values, my goals, maybe my eternity. My daydreams will tell what I really want, and perhaps what I will get, forever. Am I the hero of that hidden world, ever on stage before ghostly applause? In those daydreams, am I making conquests over enemies, money, lovers?

Or are my daydreams like Mabel's?

How do we change daydreams? Maybe it is not all that different than changing night dreams. Scrooge suspects Marley's ghost of being "a fragment of underdone potato," knowing that even in sleep, his senses are shaped by input, by context. I know this is true, having met my own version of Marley after downing a pint of Ben & Jerry's ice cream just before bedtime. I think the principle holds true in the daytime as well. For me, it has to do with decisions I make about time. If I take on the tasks of love, to care for another person, to think and talk and write about truth and goodness and beauty, to seek out those who teach me by their example and words, if I choose to do such things, then I have daydreams that I do not want to keep hidden but that I want to realize.

100

God help me, this is not who I am yet, it is only who I want to be, who I sometimes daydream to be. But I have seen enough of power and suffering to have a glimpse of the connection between the two, to see the bright thread running through the tapestry of all that I have seen back to the One who died and rose in terrible, gentle power—a power that he offers still, that I can take in only on my knees, a bit at a time, moments at a time. And moments, Mabel taught me, turn into years.

9

t and sympathy

CONSIDER (TO BEGIN) THE FOLLOWING POETIC MASTER-
piece, which my uncle taught me and which I have tried in
vain to forget:

> If ya love me, tay-toe;
> If ya don't love me, tay-toe;
> But don't teep me tittin' on the tepps
> When it's toe toad out-tied
> And I'm toe tired.

Apart from the sheer silliness here, there are several
important lessons. One is that poetry is meant to be recited
and heard, not seen on a printed page. When read aloud,
this ditty is no longer complete nonsense, but only mostly
nonsense—the plea of an anxious lover with a speech
impediment. It is also an example of *alliteration,* the technical term employed for repeated use of the same consonant. People have always liked this kind of word play and
have found that it makes things easier to remember. Or
hard to forget, as in this example. Think of Peter Piper,
who would be lost to history if we had been told only that
he "demonstrated great skill with the vegetable harvest."
    In such exaggerated examples, it is difficult to avoid silli-
ness. Because, although "P" and "T" are common letters,

after two or three careful word choices, it becomes more and more of a stretch to say anything meaningful while choosing word after word containing or beginning with the same letter. That is why the vast majority of alliteration we encounter involves no more than two or, at most, three words, and it passes almost unnoticed. Our eye or ear may be pleased momentarily, but we don't stop to consider why, to appreciate the challenge of writing something that is significant and also beautiful. The technique is tried and true but fading fast.

Consider the modern revisions of church prayer books, hymn books, and the King James Version of the Bible. Granted, the originals are sometimes archaic, but attempts to update often sacrifice the beauty of the language. The Church of England prayer book, for example, once asked forgiveness for sins arising from the "devices and desires of our own hearts." The updated version reads "*schemes* and desires of our own hearts," apparently because a committee judged that people today understand "scheming" better than "devising" or may confuse "devices" with "machines." Fair enough, but why not make an effort to retain the beauty and balance of the original, perhaps with something like "forgive us for our sinful schemes and selfish dreams"? Or, to take an example from the Bible itself, have we gained anything by replacing God's communication to Elijah in a "still small voice" (1 Kings 19:12) with "faint murmuring sound" (RSV) or "sound of sheer silence" (NRSV)?

Alas and alack, alliteration has fallen on hard times. Apart from formal poetry, which most people find too highbrow, attention to the sound and look of words is rare. In both written and verbal communication today, the intent is to get the idea across as simply as possible to accommodate low reading levels and gender or political concerns. We live in practical times.

103

Style and Substance in the New Testament

Interestingly enough, the New Testament period also saw a decline of interest in "impractical" literary techniques. Three centuries earlier, Greek philosophers like Aristotle demonstrated a fascination for language, even subdividing the category of alliteration into a half dozen or more specific forms. The best writers could construct phrases and sentences making use of related vowel or consonant sounds and initial or final or internal letters—all of this while communicating important ideas. But over time, under the domination of the excessively practical Romans, the "science of rhetoric" was neglected, and by the first century A.D. only a few highly literary types employed such advanced writing techniques.

Enter the New Testament, written in *koine* ("common") Greek by men with a mission, not by poets or philosophers. For the most part, these writers had little formal education, and even the notable exception Paul acquired his learning from Jews, not Greeks. All these factors suggest that we would be wasting our time looking for anything poetic or fancy in a book written "for the people."

Readers of the previous chapters, however, will not be shocked to learn that New Testament writers who could be so careful and subtle with their presentation of events and ideas also at times exercised great care and creativity with language. This might be expected of the one Gentile author, Luke, whose high literary style and large vocabulary comes through even in English translation of his Gospel and Acts. The level of Paul's writing varies, which is understandable given his habit of writing collaboratively or through *amanuenses* (writing secretaries, sometimes with considerable editorial freedom). Peter, too, appears to have employed Sylvanus (1 Peter 5:12), with the result that a letter from a simple Galilean fisherman turns out to be a piece of literary, highly-polished Greek prose.

The consensus of scholars, however, is that the anonymous Letter to the Hebrews is the most elegant and sophisticated of early Christian writings. Lost in translation are scores of poetic flourishes, all demonstrating mastery of the language without detracting from the content. Like a master chef who understands the importance of *presentation* for a fine entree, the writer of Hebrews offers readers the best cut of meat arranged amid the most pleasing garnishes on the finest china. Indeed, this analogy is fitting, for in chapter five he admonishes readers who *need milk, not solid food* to consider carefully his complex and challenging words, because *solid food is for the mature.* He takes them from oatmeal to steak, but he also takes them from Denny's to The Ritz.

Who is this person and why does he write this way? Scholars have not been able to agree on an author from among many options. Paul's traveling companions Apollos and Barnabas are among the most popular candidates, but we have no other writings from them to compare. The early church ascribed the letter to Paul after some debate, but even allowing for an *amanuensis,* the themes and vocabulary are a poor match, and almost no scholars today associate the letter with Paul. These problems should not cause a concern about the book's legitimate place among the New Testament writings, for which the primary criterion is authorship by an apostle or associate. Whoever this person was, he wrote with authority and associated with Christian leaders in Jerusalem and Rome (13:23–24)—factors that point only in the direction of an apostle or associate. Certainly, after Romans, this letter comprises the clearest and most profound explanation of Christianity in the first century, addressing powerfully the significance of Jesus in relation to the Old Testament and the implications of

Jesus' sacrifice for Christian living. All this is done with a flourish, employing a rich vocabulary and poetic patterns of expression.

It would be interesting to learn more about this mysterious master of both substance and style, but it is more important to appreciate his accomplishment. One particular verse pulls all of this together in a manner that is nothing short of amazing.

The Shape of Truth

Before I reveal and explain this verse, I must step away from the Greeks for a moment and explain something about the Jews. This is, after all, the letter to the *Hebrews*—a title added later but accurately reflecting the contents, which address the relationship between Jesus and the Jewish Scriptures and religion.

For many Jews, then and now, interest in and veneration for the sacred text extends beyond the content to the physical object itself. Most of us have observed Orthodox Jews dancing around the Torah scrolls in joy, for God's word is a great gift. This may help to explain why even the shapes of letters are believed to have significance. For example, the letter *beth* (ב) was called by the rabbis "the first letter of creation." This is not because it occurs first (*aleph* precedes it in the alphabet) but because Genesis begins with the words *b'reshith bara,* "in the beginning [God] created." Both words begin with *beth,* and together they refer to the power of God to create by speaking. The rabbis saw it as no accident that the shape of the letter ב is an open, speaking mouth.

Although fascination with the shapes and significance of letters peaked in the Jewish cabalistic tradition of the middle ages, there is evidence that such interest was present from the earliest times. How does this relate to Hebrews? It is evident that the early Christians, perhaps Jewish Christians in particular, were interested in the shapes of letters too. Especially the letter shaped like a cross, the Greek *tau* (T).

The *Tau* and the Cross

In the first few centuries of the Christian era, the cross was not often employed as a Christian symbol because in that culture it was an obscenity. Centuries of seeing crosses as church ornaments and jewelry have blinded us to the view people had in Roman times of writhing, screaming victims, of bodies suspended above roadways in various stages of decomposition. We might imagine the oddity of a noose or an electric chair as a religious symbol, but we have no experience of the slow and public executions that characterized Roman justice. The early Christians understandably found the cross to be an enormous public relations problem, and while they could hardly avoid reference to it in the Gospel story, they were slow to adopt it as decor. Instead, inscriptions in the catacombs and other places of early Christian art depict symbols such as the fish, anchor, shepherd, or sheaf of wheat.

The cross itself was sometimes presented in a kind of code, often combined with other symbols and allusions, such as a Tree of Life, the mast of Jonah's ship, the top of the anchor, or a serpent on a standard. When the cross did become popular, the *tau* shape (T) was rare compared to the Latin cross (†) and the Greek cross (✚). These shapes predate Christianity and do not indicate the shape of the cross on which Jesus died. We do not know precisely what kind of cross that was, but we know that Roman crucifixion took a variety of forms, including both the attachment

107

of a crosspiece just below the top of a pole, which would look more like the familiar Latin cross; and the attachment of a crosspiece at the top of a pole, which would look more like the Greek letter *tau*. The Gospels make reference to an inscription containing Jesus' mock title "King of the Jews," which artists usually portray above his head on a Latin cross. Only Luke specifies that the location was "over him," but this could mean "around his neck." In any case, the significance of the letter's shape does not depend on the precise form of Jesus' crucifixion; it is simply the letter which closely resembles the instrument of his death.

Jewish graves from the first two centuries A.D. may associate a letter of the Hebrew alphabet with Christ and the cross. During the first century, the Hebrew letter *taw* was written in the shape of a Greek cross (X or +). It is possible, therefore, that some *taw* inscriptions in Palestinian tombs may be Christian symbols depicting the cross to signify Christ. Of course, these inscriptions employ the Hebrew *taw* and not the Greek *tau*. But the Hebrew *taw* was understood as a sign of divine protection among the Jews, and it is only a small shift from that idea to the cross (and so to the Greek *tau*) as a sign of divine protection for Christians. In fact, this very connection is made in the book of Revelation (7:3; 9:4; 14:1), where salvation is given to those with the mark of the Lamb or the Father on their foreheads in wording similar to that of the Old Testament text on which Jews based their practice with the Hebrew *taw* (Ezek. 9:4–6). Scholars speculate that some early Christians may have actually marked or tattooed their foreheads in order to bear witness to their faith.

There is other evidence in Christian writings of the period. In the early second century, the church leader Justin (*Apology* 1.55.12) remarks that "nothing in the world can exist or form a whole without this sign of the cross," and he goes on

108

to cite *tau*-shapes as examples: sails, ploughs, tools, the human figure with arms outstretched, the human brow and nose, and trophy banners. A more explicit reference appears in the early-second-century Epistle of Barnabas 9:8:

> For it says, "And Abraham circumcised from his household eighteen men and three hundred." What then was the knowledge that was given to him? Notice that he first mentions the eighteen, and after a pause the three hundred. The eighteen is I (= ten) and H (= 8)—you have Jesus—and because the cross was destined to have grace in the T he says "and three hundred" [NB: The first two letters in the Greek spelling of "Jesus" are I and H; T is the Greek symbol for 300]. So he indicated Jesus in the two letters and the cross in the other.

The Sound of a Cross

This text establishes a connection for early Christians between the Greek *tau* and the cross symbol. Now at last we are ready to ask, What does all this have to do with Hebrews? The answer is contained in part of a single verse, Hebrews 2:14b. The author has just explained that Jesus took on human flesh because he wanted to share our nature. He continues, *so that through death he might destroy the one who has the power of death, that is, the devil.* In English translation there is nothing remarkable about the style of this statement, but in terms of content, it is one of the two or three most important statements in the New Testament. In these few words Christianity introduces a profound, history-changing, life-changing, unique idea: God responds to the most basic human problem, death, not by avoiding it, or transcending it, or drugging it—but by *transforming* it. And God does that not by some abstract thought or helpful pronouncement, but by true sympathy (literally, "to

109

suffer with"). God himself suffers. Death is the answer to death. Our suffering is *crossed out* by his.

At this point you may need to recall the lesson of my uncle's rhyme and read the transliteration out loud, because it is the sound that gives away the secret. I have written the Greek phonetically, and I have capitalized the T's here to draw attention to the sound and the shape—remember that our uppercase T is the same shape as the Greek *tau*.

hinna dea Too TannaToo	*so that through death*
kaTargaysay Ton To kraTos ekonTa Too TannaToo	*he might destroy the one who has the power of death,*
TooT esTin Ton diabollon	*that is, the devil.*

Here are twelve consecutive words that begin with or contain at least one T-sound (counting ten *taus* and two *thetas*, which were pronounced like *taus*), altogether fifteen T-sounds in the space of only twenty-three syllables. The staccato repetition would be as obvious to an ancient audience as to a modern one, and of course that is how the early Christians encountered it, read aloud in churches.

Coincidence or Design?

Several questions follow. Is *tau* simply a common letter in Greek, such that this sort of thing might happen every now and then by accident? Could this be a coincidence, the result of words essential to the author's line of thought? And if it is done on purpose, would the writer and the audience notice the remarkable coincidence between the cross-shaped letter and the content of the statement?

The first two questions are easy enough to answer. T is a common letter in Greek as it is in English, and shorter concentrations occur by design in a few literary works—but nothing like this. As a coincidence, fifteen T's in twenty-three syllables is almost impossible. And of course there are no coincidences for an author like this one whose work one scholar of rhetoric called "a kind of melody in words." If he didn't like the effect, he could find synonyms without T's, or he could insert other words to break up the string.

But in fact, the opposite appears to be the case. That is, the writer of Hebrews had plenty of choices for other words but chose the "T option" every time. The first word in the string (a definite article, transliterated as *too*) and the phrase "that is" (*toot estin*) are expendable, and the words "destroy" (*katargaysay*) and "power" (*kratos*) are rare synonyms for common non-T words.

I can't help wondering how the passage took shape. I picture an elderly man at a table with pen in hand, a page of scratch papyrus before him. He is thinking about a way to make the point that the death of Jesus answers our fear of death. He writes the word "death" (*tannatoo*) twice in a short space, and the sight or sound catches his attention. "This is the *cross!*" he says to himself. And he wonders, and he rejoices, and he begins to consult the treasure (Greek: *thesaurus*) of his talented literary mind for synonyms and additional touches until he comes to the final form that we have now. Then he leans back and smiles, imagining the effect when this is read aloud and the audience "gets it."

Did they get it? It is difficult to say: early church writers left no commentary on this passage. As time marched on, the practice of reading aloud declined. Scholars were not interested in style but in doctrines, and before long the Bible was read almost exclusively in Latin and other translations. Thus this remarkable sign of the cross in Hebrews 2:14 was buried and hidden for centuries.

The writer's accomplishment is just as astounding today, unearthed in the neon light of a very different world. Whatever the language, it is extremely difficult to encapsulate a great truth about God in just a few words. And in any language, it is next to impossible to come up with anything more than a silly ditty like my uncle's when using the same consonant a dozen or more times in a sentence. What this person wrote, and the skill with which he wrote it, can only be called *inspired*—in all the best senses of that word.

Although I doubt that any poet could match the original of Hebrews 2:14, it is a shame that so much of it is lost in translation. With that in mind, I offer an amateur attempt to render the verse's combination of poetry, theology, and hidden meaning:

> Through death he was to pay the cost
> For all who were to death's power lost;
> Ah, devil, you've been double crossed!

Repeating the Sound

It is unfortunate that modern interest in practical communication deafens so many of us to the beauty of the sounds of words. God speaks of himself through the created world, which we encounter through sights and sounds—not only waterfalls and songbirds, but human voices. Through his human instruments God can deliver both the truth of beauty and the beauty of truth, as he does in Hebrews 2:14. Nor does he stop there, but continues to incarnate his love over the centuries in the works of great artists, musicians, and poets. Certain recent historical developments, however, have led many Christians to forget that God loves not only with substance but also with style. I rather doubt that an explanation of *too tannatoo katargaysay,* etc., will top them from tittin' on the tepps. But we do what we can, word by word. In the beginning was the Word, in the end will be the Word, and everything in between somehow rhymes.

10

eternity: no day at the beach

IT WAS JUST A LITTLE CREEK, NO MORE THAN FIFTEEN feet wide. The horses pulling a hay wagon bolted and plunged into a creek swollen to frigid rapids by snow melt from the nearby mountains. Everyone jumped off the wagon just in time. Almost everyone. A nine-year-old girl and her mother, clinging to the wagon and to each other, were thrown into the water and then swept apart by the current. The mother was later found face down on the bank in shock. The little girl paddled desperately for a hundred, two hundred yards, past the outstretched hand of one would-be rescuer, and then she was taken under. It all took place in less than a minute. Her body was found downstream a few hours later. Her name was Susanna. She was my only child.

I thought I knew something about loss after both my marriage and career ended in the space of a year. I had read many books and written parts of this one, books exploring the significance of suffering. I was attempting to accept responsibility for my own serious failures, trying to pick up the pieces of my life for my daughter's sake. Then I found myself standing by a grave with the pieces falling from my hands. Why hold on? She was gone. We adored each other, this remarkable child and this flawed but devoted father. Susanna was affectionate, wise, funny, brilliant, a delight to all who knew her, young and old. Then one evening a telephone call came with the news that she would not come home. She would not get off the airplane the next day and run into my arms. She would not tell me about her vacation, or tell me anything, ever again. Never again would I hear that one precious word, "Daddy," spoken in her breathy little-girl voice. She would never read another book, or ride her bike, or celebrate her tenth birthday, or go out on a date, or grow to womanhood. I had thought I understood something about loss, but no other kind of experience, no book on suffering, no worst-case imagining, not even the death of other loved ones—*nothing* can prepare a person for this. Now I know something about loss.

It was only a little creek. Water. Days before she died we had played in the ocean, floated in the jacuzzi, took turns singing in my oversized shower. For us, water meant fun, not death.

A writer once made a sneering reference to Santa Barbara, the resort town where I live, as the place where people never die. It is almost too beautiful: perpetual springtime, beach and mountains and parks and gated estates and exclusive shops and posh restaurants for the privileged. And everywhere, water. Pools, fountains, mountain streams; and the ocean, visible from thousands of "view properties." Water lit by diamond-sparkling sunshine all year long. Where people never die.

Susanna is buried on a bluff overlooking the ocean. The cemetery is old, and there are not many visitors. I go there often, looking out toward some islands from a granite bench on which is carved a single word: WAITING. I listen to the ocean sigh, and the sound has become for me like breathing—the breath of the world. The creation groans

115

with us, according to St. Paul, waiting for its redemption. *And not only the creation, but we ourselves, who have the first fruits of the Spirit, groan inwardly while we wait for adoption, the redemption of our bodies* (Rom. 8:23). I begin to understand this now, this groaning, this waiting. I also begin to understand water.

Several years ago I was struck by the contrast between my seaside paradise and the vision of eternity in the last book of the Bible. *Then I saw a new heaven and a new earth; for the first heaven and the first earth had passed away, and the sea was no more* (Rev. 21:1). No more sea? What is so paradisiacal about that? If we get a new heaven and a new earth, why not a new sea, maybe one without jellyfish and moray eels? Or should we simply ascribe this vision to the perspective of an ancient landlocked people for whom the sea represented invaders and danger? In any case, the book of Revelation is obscure, and there are enough people around claiming expertise about things that haven't happened yet—why add to the speculation? My curiosity generated one academic article, and there I let the matter of the future rest.

Until now. Because for me, now, it is more personal. If the message of the Bible about an afterlife and eternity was for me only, I could be content with a variation on Pascal's famous wager, the notion that if I die and turn out to be right about Christianity, hallelujah; and if I'm wrong, well, it was a wonderful group of people to be wrong with, and a satisfying life. Besides, I was too busy living life from day to day to speculate about such things, and living life was the main point anyway: when Jesus talked about being ready, he talked about a way of living in readiness, not about knowing precisely what would happen and when.

But the loss of my only child changed all that. For the first time in my life, I really wanted to know what happens when we die—what happened when *Susanna* died. Where is she, and will we be reunited? In the agony of those first few days, I wrote in my journal that "I will not accept the expedient lie—if that is what faith is—to comfort me in my pain." I want comfort, but I want it to be true, not merely comforting. I want to go beyond hope to certainty. At first, I pleaded with God for a visitation from Susanna or some other kind of extraordinary assurance that she is in God's presence and that I will see her again. I knew from the start that there is no guarantee of any such assurance and that I would be prone to second-guess the experience anyway. Still, it didn't seem too much to ask. She was my life. Would it cost God so much just to give me a little glimpse? Couldn't he see that after all my losses and after this one unimaginably terrible loss, it might salvage my life to give me something that I could hold on to for hope? No deal. God is silent, except as he continues to reveal himself through the words he gave long ago and through the loving people who continue to wrap a heartbroken parent in their care. Those are huge exceptions, but most of the time they do not satisfy me. It may be that nothing will truly satisfy me but to die and find Susanna again. The hope that she lives on the other side of death is strong in me, and it gives direction to my life now. The alternative is to give in to despair, and then death wins, then the flood closes over my head. Water again.

Water is a parable, a metaphor, and what the Bible says about it should be received as a poem or a song, not as a series of theological propositions. Its course flows from the inaccessible past of creation to the symbolic language of the future, with a hundred backwaters and side streams in between. My way here follows the main channel, which has to do with the meaning of the sea, with death and life. If it seems a bit academic at points, remember that I am a

117

scholar, but remember too that death and life are with me in every word. This matters.

The Cube Community

At the very end of Revelation, the writer (according to tradition, the apostle John) offers the only detailed depiction of heaven in the Bible, but he does so in such a stylistic manner that it is hard to separate symbol from description. Centuries of imagination and speculation, enhanced by powerful visual images in paintings and films, offer us depictions of white-robed people sitting on clouds or strolling in a riverside glade, reminiscing with loved ones, strumming hymns on harps, conversing with saints or angels or Jesus himself. Some elements of the popular image—streets of gold, perpetual sunshine, pearly gates, a river, white robes—are taken from the Bible, and others are no more than our most hopeful human imaginings.

If we were to create an "artist's reconstruction" based on the text of Revelation, the result would be far removed from the family reunion in a park that most of us long for. Instead, we would see a jewel-encrusted, cube-shaped city, fifteen hundred miles on a side, called the New Jerusalem. But the precious metals and jewels, the mind-boggling and precise dimensions measured in multiples of twelve, are not intended for future generations of illustrators. Rather, the whole description signifies unity, community, and order brought by God out of the botched job people have made of culture. The idea is not to describe a place but to depict humanity redeemed. In other words, the New Jerusalem is a depiction of people as place, not a place for people.

The fantastic nature of this symbolism may be strange to a modern audience, but the point is profound and wonderful. God does not undo civilization or culture in the end by sending us back, each to a separate garden. Instead, he *completes* culture by bringing us together in a perfect "city" characterized by purity and order and harmony and peace. These are of course the very things we now escape cities to seek. But we can't escape ourselves, we can't get back to the garden, and we take our chaos with us everywhere. That is the flip side of all this, and it brings us back eventually to the sea. But we get there by passing through another city, an evil one.

New Jerusalem and Babylon

Jerusalem is not the only symbolic city in Revelation. Babylon is the other important place, in many ways the symbolic opposite of New Jerusalem. Of course, the historical city of Babylon had been a Mesopotamian ruin for centuries by the time Revelation was written, but the name was still in vogue as code for the corrupt world order. In John's time, that world order was embodied in a particular political power centered in Rome. But whatever John thought about the nearness of the events he predicted, his depiction of opposition to God transcends his times and takes in all of humanity in rebellion. He employs Babylon as a symbol, but also a whore, a dragon, and *the sea,* all metaphors intertwined with each other and with centuries of Jewish history. The point is not to sort out the chronology or the politics or even the meaning of every symbol, but to see an essential contrast between the chaotic forces opposed to God and the promise that God will one day order and redeem humanity. This, in a nutshell, is the contrast between Babylon and New Jerusalem. But there is more water here than a nutshell's worth, and I return to that symbol.

119

The Sea, Chaos, and Enemies

Revelation depicts the "whore of Babylon," a powerful image of humanity in rebellion against God, as sitting on "many waters" (Rev. 17:1) or on a beast that rises from the sea (Rev. 13:1), and in league with a dragon whose mouth emits a destructive flood (Rev. 12:15). To understand this imagery of the end of time, we must go all the way back to the beginning and to the ancient view of the created world.

In the first few sentences of Genesis, God overcomes the formless waste by "gathering" the waters and establishing the earth and sky above them. Ancient people pictured a three-tiered universe with the heaven and earth perched atop a seething, unstable chaos. God "contains" this mess, he rules over it, but he does not transform it. It remains a place of disorder, and eventually it becomes a metaphor for those in opposition to God, for the enemies of God's people. A few examples from the Old Testament illustrate this progression.

God's containment of the sea sometimes portrays the sea almost as having a mind of its own, and a hostile one at that: *He assigned to the sea its limit, so that the waters might not transgress his command* (Prov. 8:29). *I placed the sand as a boundary for the sea, a perpetual barrier that it cannot pass; though the waves toss, they cannot prevail, though they roar, they cannot pass over it* (Jer. 5:22).

In the story of the Exodus of Israel, the sea is treated not only as a physical barrier but as God's enemy: *He rebuked the Red Sea, and it became dry; he led them through the deep as through a desert* (Ps. 106:9). Interestingly, the human enemy of Israel, Pharoah's army, is in one passage described in the same terms as the sea: the Israelites pass through, *the waters forming a wall for them on their right and on their left* (Exod. 14:22). They later praise God because Pharoah's soldiers *became as still as a stone until your people, O Lord, passed by* (Exod. 15:16). Here water is an enemy and the enemy is like water. It must be contained, made still, dried up.

Such an identification between the ocean or flood waters and the enemies of God becomes common in the Old Testament. These enemies may be personal or political opponents of God's people. God is praised because *You silence the roaring of the seas, the roaring of their waves, the tumult of the peoples* (Ps. 65:7); similarly, *He reached down from on high, he took me; he drew me out of mighty waters. He delivered me from my strong enemy, and from those who hated me; for they were too mighty for me* (Ps. 18:16–17). A prophecy of a coming invasion begins, *Thus says the Lord: See, waters are rising out of the north and shall become an overflowing torrent; they shall overflow the land and all that fills it, the city and those who live in it* (Jer. 47:2).

There is one more step in this development. Because the threat of personal and political enemies is very close to the threat of death, flood waters or the sea become an image of the place of the dead (the Pit, Sheol, Abaddon) or of death itself. Here water is an image of terror:

> I call upon the Lord, who is worthy to be praised, and I am saved from my enemies. For the waves of death encompassed me, the torrents of perdition assailed me; the cords of Sheol entangled me, the snares of death confronted me.
>
> 2 Samuel 22:4–6

> The shades below tremble, the waters and their inhabitants. Sheol is naked before God, and Abaddon has no covering.
>
> Job 26:5–6

> Save me, O God, for the waters have come up to my neck. I sink in deep mire, where there is no foothold; I have come into deep waters, and the flood sweeps over me. Rescue me from sinking in the mire; let me be delivered from my ene-

121

mies and from the deep waters. Do not let the flood sweep over me, or the deep swallow me up, or the Pit close its mouth over me.

Psalm 69:1–2, 14–15

I called to the Lord out of my distress, and he answered me; out of the belly of Sheol I cried, and you heard my voice. You cast me into the deep, into the heart of the seas, and the flood surrounded me; all your waves and your billows passed over me. Then I said, "I am driven away from your sight; how shall I look again upon your holy temple?" The waters closed in over me.

Jonah 2:2–5a

The sea, primordial chaos, death, the abode of the dead, sea monsters, and the human enemies of God are realities so closely linked in the minds of Jewish writers as to be interchangeable in some instances. By the time we reach Revelation, we should not be surprised that the angel explains the imagery to the prophet in this way: *And he said to me, "The waters that you saw, where the whore is seated, are peoples and multitudes and nations and languages"* (Rev. 17:15). Nor should we be surprised to see the enemies of God, including finally *death itself,* thrown into a "lake of fire" (Rev. 19:20; 20:10; 20:14–15).

Sea Imagery in Revelation

The Book of Revelation fairly drips with water imagery. The fifty-plus references comprise by far the greatest concentration of such imagery in the Bible or in other literature of that time. The collection of images is dizzying, but take a deep breath as I plunge through them to convey an overall sense of the sea as something other than a body of water.

A dragon, symbolic enemy of God, takes his place by the sea (12:18), from which he calls up a beast to lead a rebellion (13:1). The dragon is the sea monster Leviathan (Isa. 27:1), who, according to the Old Testament, is reduced to carrion after judgment (Ps. 74:13–14). In Revelation it is rebellious people who become carrion (19:17–21) while the dragon is temporarily bound (20:2) prior to his ultimate demise in the lake of fire (20:10), where he is joined by rebellious humanity, dredged up from Hades and the sea (20:13). Babylon sits on the beast (17:3) but also sits on "many waters" (17:1). The beast ascends from the sea (13:1) but also from the bottomless pit (11:7; 17:8); and while he sits on a throne that is in fact the beast's throne (13:2), he actually *is* the throne—that is, the mount—of the whore (17:3). The beast's seven heads and ten horns are interpreted as specific kings (17:9–13), but later these kings are distinguished from the beast (17:16) and still later generalized as all humanity deceived by the beast (19:20)—or the dragon (20:3, 10). This deception is perpetrated by frog-like demons emanating from the dragon, the beast, and the beast's prophet (15:13–14). In 12:15, it is the dragon who vomits a river of persecution; but in 11:7 and 13:7 it is the beast who makes war on the saints. Are you ready for a quiz over all of this? If these overlapping images are not themselves sufficient to muddy the waters, it might also be asked in nearly every case if the images refer to individuals, political groups, religious groups, or demonic forces. Is the confusion hopeless?

This much is evident. The imagery is too clearly tied to human political and economic activity to make sense as an attack on religious or demonic powers, but it is too general to fit any particular period of history, including the obvious choice, first century Rome. The dragon and the beast and the maritime commerce described in chapter 18 all point toward the Roman empire, but the imagery is generalized throughout Revelation to include "peoples and multitudes and nations and languages" as the ultimate sea of God's enemies. Rome is merely a symptom, not the disease, and that may be one reason Revelation names only the defunct Babylon. Desire for the pleasures of this world and susceptibility to deception do not end with the fall of Rome. Finally it is all humanity which rises like a tide against the Lord and then falls back hissing into the lake of fire.

But the image of fire introduces yet another problem. Where is *water* in this incongruous connection between the (presumably wet) sea and the lake of fire or smoking bottomless pit that spawns the beast and into which the forces of evil are thrown in the end? There is no contradiction if we understand that the terms and descriptions of Sheol, Gehenna, Hades, and the Abyss are like illustrations by different artists of the same idea. Whether the images share features or seem contradictory, they all contribute to an understanding of things beyond our earthly comprehension—the place of the dead, the abode of demons, the focal point of opposition to God. So it is that whether we picture a fiery pit or a heaving sea, we are given a glimpse of the end of chaos. In effect, the snake is made to swallow itself, and it doesn't matter much whether the last terrible noise is a slurp or a sizzle. The point is that chaos cannot be changed—it must be eliminated. Likewise, death and the forces that represent it must be eliminated. In the end, the imperfect must make way if the perfect community is to exist. "Mostly perfect" makes no sense.

I do not intend to speculate about hell and judgment. My purpose is to understand why the author of Revelation predicted what no one else had up to that time: the ultimate disappearance of the sea. He stresses contrasts. The New Jerusalem is an extension of the believing community; Babylon and its demise are an extension of humanity in opposition to God. The present world order inexorably collapses on itself; the new community descends gracefully onto the new earth, an image of perfect order. Death, represented most vividly as a churning sea contained but never conquered, is replaced by *the river of the water of life, bright as crystal, flowing from the throne of God and of the Lamb through the middle of the street of the city* (Rev. 22:1). Chaos gives way to order, isolation to community, death to life. And water gives way to water, but now it is the water of life.

The Death of Jesus and the Birth of Hope

This chapter may appear incongruous in a book on the death of Jesus, but there is a connection that is more than coincidence. In chapter 5 of Revelation, just as the predictions of the end of time are about to begin, there is a dramatic moment when the prophet begins to weep because a certain scroll must be read and no one is found who is worthy. Just then there appears *a Lamb standing as if it had been slaughtered,* and those gathered around the throne of God sing a new song, proclaiming that the Lamb is worthy, he can open the scroll, the wonderful future can unfold.

What an extraordinary image. A lamb, a timid domestic beast—and one bearing the marks of death—is the conquering hero who ushers in eternity. Repetition drives the point home: there is a handful of references elsewhere in the New Testament to Jesus as a lamb, but from here onward in Revelation, that is his title almost exclusively, occurring twenty-eight times. By this one word the prophet conveys a critical truth. For all the power described by the prophet in and around the throne of God, only the gentle one who has willingly suffered can move events to their completion. For the last time and forever, it is only a death that answers death, it is only a Lamb who can defeat the Dragon. Only the Lamb can wash the robes of his people clean with blood (Rev. 7:14), only he can guide his people through through the great ordeal, the chaos of the sea, and guide them to springs of the water of life (Rev. 7:17). Only the Lamb can give hope.

Postscript

It matters to me that this is true, not merely interesting, not merely comforting. The chaos of this life, the flood waters, have closed over my head. Yet I choose against despair. I believe that death will die one day, that the love of God will prevail. In the meantime, even if the rest of my path lies in shadow, I will follow the Lamb in trust and in hope—until I see Susanna again. It may be that faith is no more and no less than a choice between the words "it may be so" and "I will live as if it is so."

Not far from my apartment, on a bluff overlooking the heaving sea, there is a marker on a new grave that bears the name of my only child and the following inscription:

With joy still deeper than pain
Gently flows the River
Where we shall meet again.

Acknowledgments

Some of the essays in this volume are adaptations of previous scholarly articles and other publications by the author. Readers interested in more detailed treatments and documentation of the technical aspects of this material may wish to read further.

Chapter 2, "The Womb, the Tomb, and the Curtained Room," is adapted from "Divine Revelation and Penetration of Barriers in the Gospels," *Novum Testamentum* XXIV 3 (1992): 229–46.

Chapter 3, "The Man Who Would Be God," is adapted from "Mark 15:16–32: The Crucifixion Narrative and the Roman Triumphal Procession," *New Testament Studies* 41/1 (January 1995): 1–18.

Chapter 5, "Jesus Goes to Therapy," borrows from ideas developed in "Cry of Dereliction or Cry of Judgment: Mark 15:34 in Context," *Bulletin for Biblical Research* 4 (1994): 145–53.

Chapter 6, "The God in the Garden," appeared first in *Ministry* (March 2001): 22–24.

Chapter 8, "On Death and Power and One Old Lady," is a revision of "Conclusion: Getting There From Here," in *Trying to Be Good* (Grand Rapids: Zondervan, 1990), 179–88.

Chapter 9, "*T* and Sympathy," is adapted from "The Tau as the Cross: Ornament and Content in Hebrews 2:14," *Biblica* 76/1 (1995): 75–84.

Chapter 10, "Eternity: No Day at the Beach," is adapted from "And the Sea Was No More: Water as People, Not Place," in *To Tell the Mystery*, ed. T. Schmidt and M. Silva (Sheffield: Sheffield Academic Press, 1994), 233–49.